W9-APD-624

Homeowner's Guide to Wood Refinishing

David Schansberg

Ideals Publishing Corp.
Milwaukee, Wisconsin

Table of Contents

ISBN 0-8249-6124-2

Copyright © 1982 by Ideals Publishing Corporation

Published by Ideals Publishing Corporation
11315 Watertown Plank Road
Milwaukee, Wisconsin 53226

Editor, David Schansberg

Cover photo and inside photos by Jerry Koser. All finishing materials courtesy of Elm Grove Ace Hardware. Special thanks to Naked Furniture, Milwaukee.

⌂ SUCCESSFUL
HOME IMPROVEMENT SERIES

Bathroom Planning and Remodeling
Kitchen Planning and Remodeling
Space Saving Shelves and Built-ins
Finishing Off Additional Rooms
Finding and Fixing the Older Home
Money Saving Home Repair Guide
Homeowner's Guide to Tools
Homeowner's Guide to Electrical Wiring
Homeowner's Guide to Plumbing
Homeowner's Guide to Roofing and Siding
Homeowner's Guide to Fireplaces
Home Plans for the '80s
Planning and Building Home Additions
Homeowner's Guide to Concrete and Masonry
Homeowner's Guide to Landscaping
Homeowner's Guide to Swimming Pools
Homeowner's Guide to Fastening Anything
Planning and Building Vacation Homes
Homeowner's Guide to Floors
Home Appliance Repair Guide
Homeowner's Guide to Wood Refinishing
Children's Rooms and Play Areas
Wallcoverings: Paneling, Painting, and Papering

Wood: What It Is — What It Does

Anyone who has recently shopped for furniture and compared features and prices has probably developed an appreciation for the value of quality solid wood products. Because of the considerable time and effort some manufacturers and craftsmen spend in creating their products, furniture, cabinetry, and moldings made of solid wood are expensive.

Wood has long been a respected and highly desirable building product because it has a unique beauty and feel that only nature and time can create. The rich tone and color of a finely crafted piece of wood furniture stands out in a showroom of imitation and inferior products of similar design. One can distinguish the subtle textures of the grain by simply passing a hand over the surface. Grasp the edge of the solid wood piece of furniture and lift; if it seems to have taken root, it is likely to be constructed of solid hardwood.

Wood is an impressive, versatile material, but much of the appeal and beauty is created by its finish. It is hard to distinguish one wood from another in an entire showroom of unfinished and unpainted furniture without close inspection. A proper finish will blend with the style of the piece and enhance the wood's character by bringing out the natural beauty of the grain and texture. Finishing can highlight a distinctive grain pattern, give wood a much richer tone, and protect the wood from dirt and moisture. But the wood itself must possess character and inherent beauty that can be enhanced by a finish. The entire finishing process begins with and depends on the type of wood to be finished.

Whether you plan to purchase new furniture that may some day require refinishing, restore an old piece of furniture found in the attic or at an auction, build and finish your own cabinets, furniture or bookshelves, or finish a piece of "naked" furniture available at unfinished furniture stores, give careful consideration to the wood. Select a wood that best meets all your requirements; only then can you intelligently select the type of finish that will ensure the best, most attractive results.

This chapter will discuss wood in general, the various popular furniture and woodworking woods, characteristics and the finishing possibilities of each wood. Actual application techniques and instructions will be detailed in later chapters.

What Is Wood?

Most people who use and value wood have a natural curiosity about where it comes from and how various species differ. Knowing that wood comes from a tree does not fully explain why it is unique among all the natural and synthetic materials on earth. Trees, familiar as they are, are far from being completely understood. How, for example, does a tree defy gravity and lift water hundreds of feet from its roots to the topmost leaves? We still aren't sure.

All the trunk's growing takes place in a layer of cells, only one cell thick, between the wood in the tree's center and the bark. These growing cells—the cambium layer—create new sapwood on one side, new bark on the other. The sapwood cells eventually become heartwood and are continually renewed by more cell growth from the cambium.

Trees differ in the size, form, and distribution of their various types of cells. These differences account for variations among species in mechanical and physical properties, such as color, strength, aroma, decay resistance, density, and grain pattern.

Though nearly all the tree is put to good use by the lumber industry, we are concerned here with the woody part: sapwood and heartwood.

Advantages and Disadvantages of Wood

Wood is an amazing construction material with many advantages and several limitations. Below is a brief review of wood's general physical characteristics and outstanding properties.

- It is relatively light in weight in relation to its strength, making it easier to handle than many other materials.
- It can be cut and worked with simple, familiar hand tools or power tools and is easy to join with screws, nails, bolts, or other common fasteners.
- Its strength properties include exceptional impact strength, considerable dimensional stability along the grain, and good flexural rigidity which permits it to retain its properties when bent.
- It can be joined with adhesives, and research promises even greater improvement in the ability to use this characteristic.
- It resists corrosion by chemicals and has excellent insulation qualities against both heat and cold because of its fibrous structure which entraps air. It's the only commonly used thermal insulator that also has good structural qualities.
- When dry it is a poor conductor of electricity.
- It absorbs energy far better than concrete or steel,

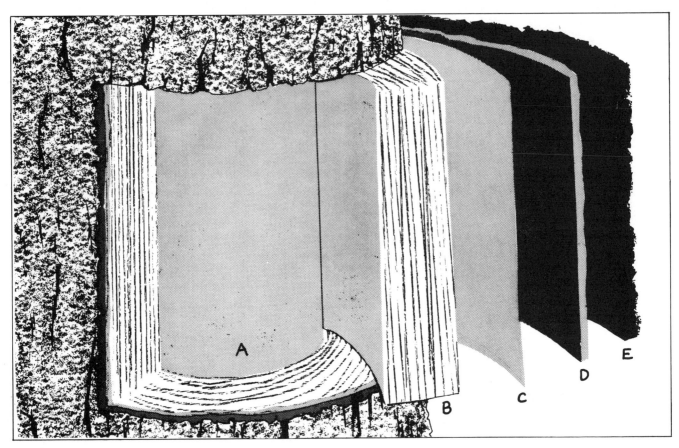

The basic layers of a tree: (A) heartwood, (B) sapwood, (C) cambium cell layer, (D) inner bark, and (E) outer bark.

so it is an excellent material for floors—easier on the feet.

- It is surprisingly durable. Beams 2,700 years old have been found in a tomb in Turkey. Centuries-old beams are still supporting Japanese temples. We see Colonial homes in New England looking much as they did 300 years ago.
- Finally, it is beautiful—and the beauty endures. In its natural state or with a manmade finish, wood appeals to man's aesthetic sense.

Naturally, wood has its limitations as well. You must work within these limits and avoid forcing wood to do something for which it is not suited.

- Wood shrinks across the grain when dried from the green condition. As noted above, it is dimensionally stable in the lengthwise direction, and length is usually the most important dimension in woodworking. This property explains why wood should be dried before manufacture. Plywood avoids this problem because each veneer layer is placed with its grain at right angles to the grain of adjoining layers, to evenly distribute tension.
- Most wood decays if exposed to moist conditions because wood-destroying fungi are able to grow. Completely saturated wood-cell cavities filled with water, however, do not decay because fungi

can get no oxygen. Wood can be treated to resist decay.

- Wood is combustible but can be a far safer material than so-called noncombustible construction materials.
- Wood may be subject to boring by insects, such as termites, but treatment can counteract this.

Wood varies in its properties and behavior in comparison with metals and synthetic materials, and may even vary within the same species. The knowledgeable woodworker learns to anticipate and compensate.

Selection of Wood

Many factors must be considered when selecting wood to finish or wood that may someday require refinishing. You may want to add a piece of furniture to an existing group. Perhaps you desire a particular stain or finish that will enhance other furnishings in the home. In any case, your choice of wood should be determined by intended use, desired results, cost, and the type of finish to be applied. For example, a dining room table can see quite a bit of activity, and the wood it is constructed of must be able to withstand heavy use. Bookshelves, on the other hand, can be made of softer woods, such as pine, gum, or fir, because they will not be subjected to daily abuse.

Mahogany, walnut, and cherry are beautiful woods but very expensive. If this cost is too prohibitive, other less expensive woods with similar character can be finished to resemble the expensive woods quite closely. To accomplish this, a thorough understanding of the various elements of a wood's character is essential. Only then can one wood be finished to look like another.

Wood is an organic material, and each wood has its own set of identifying characteristics that distinguish it from other woods. The most common characteristics are color, hardness, strength, and grain.

Color The actual shades of a wood in the raw or unfinished state are its color. Woods vary drastically in color from creamy white to dark brown or black, and from reddish tints to blue to green, often with streaks of other colors running through. Color is important, but through finishing, color can be enhanced, strengthened, or even changed.

Hardness The ability of wood to withstand shock without damage is called hardness. Woods with hard textures generally are more durable and last longer, but very hard woods are difficult to work with and may dull or damage woodworking tools. Medium hardwoods are usually preferred in furniture construction because they have the combined properties of good shock resistance and moderately easy workability.

Strength Many types of furniture, cabinet, and bookshelf designs require woods that have the strength and resiliency to be subjected to repeated stress and strain. Examples of such woods are mahogany, walnut, maple, and oak.

Grain Good grain characteristics is probably the most important factor in wood selection because there is no substitute for fine grain pattern. Stain can change the color of wood, veneers can improve hardness, and surrounding framework can increase strength. For wood to be beautiful, the inherent grain

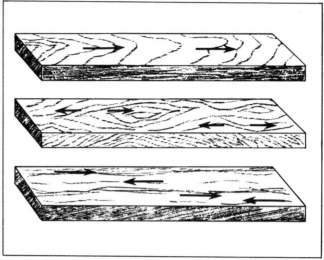

Depending on the way a log is cut, the grain of its boards can run in several patterns.

must be beautiful. The appearance of grain through the finish enhances beauty. Grain is formed by pores in the wood. The pattern these pores create in the wood is called figure. Figure can be controlled to a degree by the way boards are cut. By changing the angle at which boards are cut from the main 100, different figures are created. When pores are open and visible, the wood is open grained. Small, tightly packed pores which cannot be detected by the human eye are closed grain. Closed-grained woods generally do not require filling before finishing. Open-grained woods should be filled if a smooth finish is desired or can be left open to create a rough, rustic look.

Color, strength, hardness, and grain vary to some degree in every wood. Once these characteristics are known for a specific wood, identification is relatively easy, and the proper finish can then be applied. In the following section, general characteristics are given for the major hardwoods and softwoods used for most fine woodworking projects, and the best finishing techniques for that particular wood are recommended.

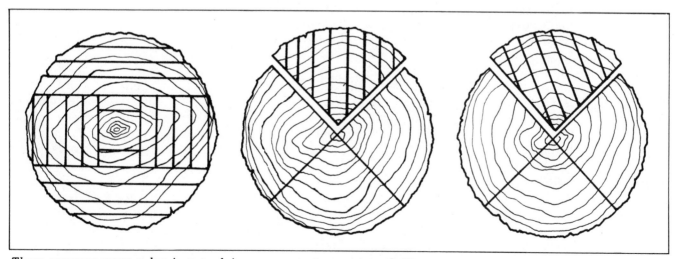

Three common ways a log is cut: plain sawn, quarter sawn, and rift sawn.

Hardwoods and Softwoods

Woods are classified in two main subdivisions—hardwoods and softwoods. Actually the terms hardwood and softwood have little correspondence to the mechanical properties of the woods, but refer, rather, to the kinds of trees they come from.

Lumbermen use hardwoods as a trade term to designate wood from flowering broad-leaved trees, while softwoods come from cone-bearing or coniferous trees, most of which have evergreen, needlelike leaves. The terms are not necessarily related to the density of the wood and how physically hard it is. It is true that most hardwoods are harder and heavier than most softwoods; but several hardwoods, e.g., yellow poplar, aspen, and balsa, are softer than some softwoods, such as Douglas fir, longleaf pine, and yew.

Another rough classification is applied to woods that are prized mainly for their appearance as opposed to those that are used as structural members, or in fine furniture terms, as primary and secondary woods. Again, though there is some overlap and many of the most handsome hardwoods are also very strong, their cost may prohibit their use except on visible surfaces. They are also usually harder to work. So we often think of hardwoods as decorative and softwoods as workhorses.

Worldwide, hundreds of species of hardwoods are harvested and marketed. Of the 500 or more separate hardwood species in the United States, about 30 may be considered of commercial importance. The primary hardwoods are walnut, mahogany, maple, oak, ash, birch, chestnut, gum and cherry. Most hardwoods are used for furniture construction and for the top, visible layer of many veneers in furniture, plywood, or paneling. Each wood has its own properties and characteristics and can therefore be finished in different ways and used in different projects.

Fewer species of softwoods are harvested than hardwoods, but the volume is much greater. In the United States about 75 percent of our sawtimber on commercial forest land is softwood, with the remaining 25 percent hardwood. Sawtimber trees are those of a size and quality suitable for harvest and manufacture into structural wood products. Softwoods include pines, fir, spruce, cedar, and redwood. These woods are, in fact, softer than most hardwoods and tend to dent and damage more easily if subjected to hard wear. Softwoods are generally less expensive than hardwoods. Most unfinished furniture is constructed of softwood.

Popular Hardwoods

Ash Native to the eastern region of the United States, particularly the Great Lakes area and New England. Heartwood is brown and sapwood is off-white. Species vary considerably in character. Distinct straight grain and

Easy Hardwood Identification Chart

Wood	Color Heartwood	Sapwood	Pattern Figure	Grain	Strength
Ash	Creamy light brown	White	Pronounced straight grain	Open	Good
Aspen	Light grayish brown	Creamy white	Fine straight grain	Closed	Poor
Basswood	Pale golden brown	Creamy white	Very faint	Closed	Poor
Beech	Reddish brown	Creamy white	Straight grain, uniform texture	Closed	Good
Birch	Light reddish brown	White	Distinct wavy or straight	Closed	Good
Butternut	Light brown	White	Faint, large pores	Open	Medium
Cherry	Reddish brown	White	Straight grain, may burl	Closed	Medium
Chestnut	Grayish brown	Creamy white	Distinct, some wormholes	Open	Medium
Ebony	Dark gray to black	Lighter	Straight grain	Open	Good
Elm	Grayish red brown	Creamy white	Distinct wavy	Open	Good
Gum	Reddish brown	Pinkish white	Very faint	Closed	Medium
Hickory	Brown	Creamy white	Pronounced close grain	Open	Good
Mahogany	Reddish brown	Creamy white	Fine texture, striped	Open	Medium
Maple	Reddish brown	White	Obscure straight grain	Closed	Good
Oak	Grayish brown	White	Prominent	Open	Good
Poplar	Yellowish brown	White	Faint	Closed	Medium
Rosewood	Dark reddish brown	White	Faint, streaked	Open	Good
Sycamore	Reddish brown	Pale reddish brown	Faint, flaked	Closed	Good
Teak	Golden brown	Light brown	Streaked	Open	Good
Walnut	Rich brown	Creamy white	Distinct striped or plain	Open	Good

coarse open pores are similar to oak. Wood is strong, heavy, hard, and stiff with high shock resistance in relation to weight. Ash is used for handles, oars, baseball bats, watertight cooperage, veneer paneling, and furniture (used extensively for framework). *FINISH:* may be finished natural with an open-pored effect. Bleaches very well. Can apply clear finish over bare wood or over stain. Where contrast is desired, use a light gray stain with a gray or white filler.

Aspen Similar to cottonwood and poplar, aspen is grown commercially in the northern Great Lakes states and Rocky Mountain regions. Heartwood is grayish white to light grayish brown, merging gradually into lighter sapwood. Wood is straight grained, has a fine uniform texture, is easy to work, lightweight, and soft with low strength. Aspen is used mainly in light structural construction, pallets, pulpwood, and particle board. *FINISH:* may be finished natural or stained with a light color. Fill with light brown filler. Bleaches well. Dull rub or polish finish.

Basswood Also known as linden, basswood is common to the northern United States and Canada. Heartwood is pale yellow brown with darker reddish markings, merging gradually into wide white sapwood. Faint growth rings and wood rays that appear slightly darker than background wood. Wood is soft, lightweight, fine, and even textured with small pores, straight grained, and easy to work. Weak wood with low resistance to shock and with shrinkage properties but does not warp in use. Basswood is used primarily for sash and door frames, woodenware, boxes, millwork, and furniture. Excellent carving wood. *FINISH:* apply clear finish over light or dark stain. Colored enamels also work well if painted furniture is desired.

Beech Common to central states and middle Atlantic states, particularly the Appalachian Mountain region. Heartwood is reddish brown, and sapwood is a creamy white. Wood is heavy, hard, strong, and highly shock resistant. Pronounced wood rays and tiny wood pores. Resembles maple in color and markings. Large shrinkage. Because beech is totally tasteless and odorless, it is commonly used for foodware and woodenware. Other uses include furniture, flooring, handles, cooperage, and railroad ties. *FINISH:* apply clear finish over natural wood or over fruitwood stains. Bleaches well and is very suitable for enamel paints. Should be dull rubbed or polished.

Birch Found extensively in the Great Lakes region, the Northeast, and in Canada with some species growing along Appalachian Mountains to Georgia. Yellow birch and paper birch have white sapwood, light reddish brown heartwood. Sweet birch has light-colored sapwood and dark reddish brown heartwood. All birch wood is heavy, hard, strong, and has excellent shock resistance. Because birch has fine uniform texture with extremely small wood pores, the wood can be easily stained to resemble other more expensive woods. Birch is used primarily for structural parts of furniture, veneers, woodenware, cooperage, boxes, and doors. Birch plywood is used in cabinets and furniture. *FINISH:* clear smooth grain presents many finishing alternatives depending on color of the wood. White birch can be finished natural, bleached, or stained to closely resemble maple. Yellow birch will take a walnut or dark stain. Brownish wood can be finished to imitate cherry or mahogany.

Butternut Also known as white walnut, butternut is found in the north-central states and southern Canada. Heartwood is brown; sapwood is narrow and nearly white with random dark streaks running throughout. Wood is moderately light in weight, soft and medium textured, not very stiff, is only moderately shock resistant, and has large open pores. Butternut is used for interior millwork, furni-

ture, cabinet veneer, and paneling. *FINISH:* may be stained in light oak or walnut colors with fillers to even out color. Can be dull rubbed or polished. A clear finish can be applied over natural wood.

Cherry Scattered from southeastern Canada throughout the eastern United States. Heartwood is light to dark reddish brown with distinctive luster and is often mistaken for mahogany. Sapwood is narrow and white. Cherry wood has a uniform, medium hard texture with straight grain and small, individual pores that are close together. The wood is moderately hard, strong, heavy, shock and wear resistant, and machines very well. It is dimensionally stable after seasoning. Cherry is used in furniture, woodenware, caskets, and fine veneer for paneling. *FINISH:* wood stains very well, especially stains with a reddish cast, such as mahogany. Because of close grain, cherry takes varnishes well. Dull or high polish. Filler not necessary. Will not bleach.

Chestnut Found in isolated areas of the eastern United States. Chestnut used to grow over wider area, but insect blight killed many trees. Standing dead timber is still harvested. Heartwood is grayish white; sapwood is white. Grain structure resembles oak, but chestnut is only moderately hard. Wood is durable, strong, and somewhat heavy. Primarily used for poles, railway ties, furniture, and many outdoor uses as solid wood or face veneer for plywood. In recent years "wormy chestnut" has become a popular furniture wood and is used in paneling, trim, and picture frames. *FINISH:* usually stained dark in Mediterranean furniture styles. Can be finished natural.

Ebony Native to the East Indies, West Indies, and Africa. Heartwood is black with a pattern of fine, light gray streaks. Wood is hard, heavy, and strong. Ebony is generally used in veneers and in inlays. *FINISH:* requires careful finishing. Wash surface with lacquer reducer, apply coat of gloss lacquer, and rub. Ebony will not bleach and can be stained, filled with a dark color, and rubbed.

Elm Limited primarily to the eastern United States. Dutch elm disease threatens the remaining trees. Heartwood is light to dark brown; sapwood is nearly white. Species vary in hardness. Wood is heavy, shock resistant, and has straight grain with well defined light and dark boundaries. Has excellent bending qualities. Generally used in boxes, barrels and furniture, particularly pieces that feature bent wood. *FINISH:* can be stained with light or dark colors; apply clear finish.

Gum (Tupelo) Abundant in the southern United States and found in many other regions. Heartwood is light brownish gray, tinged with pink, gradually merging into lighter sapwood. Gum is one of the softest woods used in furniture construction and will not tolerate hard wear. The wood has fine uniform texture, small tight pores, and distinctive grain patterns. It is moderately heavy and somewhat shock resistant but will dent if hit hard enough. Gum is also one of the cheapest furniture hardwoods, making it one of the most popular as well. Other uses include veneer, paneling, crates, and boxes. *FINISH:* gum is one of the easiest woods to finish. It takes all types of stains very well and can be finished to closely resemble other more expensive hardwoods, such as walnut and mahogany. It bleaches well and can be rubbed to give excellent results.

Hickory (Pecan) Pecan is a member of the hickory family, native to the south-central United States. Other species are found throughout the eastern United States. Heartwood is reddish brown with dark streaks; sapwood is white and thick. Wood is very heavy, hard, and strong. Pores are visible but not large enough to require a filler. Closed-grain pattern is prominent. Wood is hard on tools because of weight and high shock resistance. Pecan is becoming a favorite furniture wood and is popular in Mediterranean and provincial designs. Used for ladder rungs, tool handles, dowels, veneers, and smoking food products. *FINISH:* can be stained to resemble walnut and can be finished in any natural shade. Antiquing can create beautiful results.

Mahogany True mahogany is imported from Central America, the West Indies, South America, Africa, and Mexico. Mahogany is the Cadillac of furniture hardwoods. Heartwood is pink when cut but changes to a color ranging from light golden brown to dark reddish brown when exposed to air. Mahogany is an excellent finishing wood because it takes stains well and is easy to work. The pores are open, and the grain has excellent figure ranging from straight to wavy. The wood is dimensionally sound and can be worked into many styles. It is moderately soft yet very shock resistant. Numerous pores require filling for a smooth finish. Used in many styles of furniture and cabinets, boats, electronic cabinets, caskets, paneling, and veneers. *FINISH:* bleaches very well. When properly filled, wood will receive most lacquers, shellacs, and varnishes. To enhance wood figure, finish natural.

Maple Another favorite for fine crafted furniture and homemade furniture as well, maple grows extensively throughout the United States and Canada. Heartwood is light reddish brown; sapwood is creamy white with a slight reddish tint. Maple is one of the strongest hardwoods. The wood is hard, heavy, stiff, and very shock and split resistant. It has large shrinkage. In solid form the grain is straight with a slight wavy nondescript figure and fine, uniform texture. When cut into veneers, maple takes on more elaborate markings called bird's-eye, blister, and curly. Bird's-eye maple is rare and expensive. Maple is hard to work. Primary uses include tool handles, flooring (because of high abrasion resistance), furniture, boxes, crates, and woodenware. Many less expensive woods are finished in the traditional maple color. Do not depend on color alone for identification. *FINISH:* because of close grain, stains do not penetrate well, but with effort, it will take any kind of finish that can be rubbed to a fine gloss. Popular finishes are natural, blond, and bleached. Antique effects work well for Early American reproductions.

Oak, White and Red Is readily available throughout the United States, Canada, Europe, Asia, and Africa. Oaks account for more standing lumber than any other hardwood. Oak has been used for centuries in furniture making. It is regaining popularity once again after falling out of favor for a number of years because other popular fine-grained hardwoods, such as walnut and maple, are becoming scarce and expensive. Heartwood ranges in color from light grayish brown in the white oak group to reddish brown in the red oaks. Sapwood is white for all species. White oak is preferred for finishing because it is less permeable and more durable. Oak is heavy, hard, stiff, strong, and very resistant to decay and shock. The wood has prominent, open pores that create a striking grain figure. It is difficult wood to work, due to extreme hardness. Used for all types of furniture and cabinetry, flooring, lumber, caskets, cooperage, and boat decking. *FINISH:* large pores require filling, but oak finishes well in a variety of ways. The wide pores make it suitable for a contrasting finish. Stain can be omitted for a natural finish.

Poplar Common in the eastern half of the United States and parts of Canada. Poplar is easy to work, takes stain and paints very well, and is a popular substitute for more expensive woods. Heartwood is yellowish brown with green black or blue streaks running along the grain; sapwood is white. Wood has a soft even texture and fine straight grain with small, barely visible wood pores. Poplar is a fairly soft, weak, and lightweight wood and only somewhat shock resistant. Second growth wood is heavier and harder than old growth. Primary uses include inexpensive furniture, cabinet interiors, interior finish, siding, woodenware, plywood, and pulpwood. *FINISH:* easy to work, accepts most finishes, and can be stained to imitate popular, more expensive hardwoods, such as walnut, mahogany, and maple. Close grain enables poplar to accept paint without a filler. Enamels improve shock resistance.

Rosewood Imported from Brazil and India. This wood is rare, costly, and hard to find. Heartwood ranges from dark brown to dark purple with prominent curving blackish streaks. The wood is extremely hard and heavy with large, open wood pores, and coarse texture. Used as veneer for decorative plywood, cutlery handles, and inexpensive furniture, primarily eighteenth century reproductions. *FINISH:* wash surface thoroughly with lacquer reducer; stain with light red stain or apply clear finish over bare wood. Cannot be bleached.

Sycamore The central states are the major producers of sycamore lumber. Heartwood is pale reddish brown; sapwood is lighter shade. The wood is moderately heavy, hard, stiff, strong, and has good shock resistance. It is fine textured with small wood pores and interlocked grain in a wide growth pattern. Sycamore is used in cooperage, tool handles, hidden parts of furniture, flooring, and lumber. *FINISH:* apply clear finish over bare wood for natural look. Can be bleached or stained a light shade.

Teak Imported from India, Burma, southeastern Asia, Latin America, Africa, and Java. Teak is one of the world's most popular and valuable woods. Quality wood is expensive because of the extensive time required for proper drying and seasoning. Improperly cured teak will warp. The medium-hard wood ranges from golden brown to dark brown with fine black markings in a pattern similar to walnut. It is an oily wood with a leathery smell. Wood is heavy, strong, and tough with a high degree of natural durability. It is moderately easy to work, but the silica content can cause tools to dull. Major uses are ship building, furniture, parquet flooring, decorative carvings, plywood, and paneling. *FINISH:* surface must be washed with lacquer reducer because of high oil content. Can be finished natural by applying clear finish over bare wood, or use a walnut filler, then seal and lacquer. Glaze to fill cracks. Dull rub or polish.

Walnut Considered to be one of the highest quality fine hardwoods because of its versatility and natural even grain. The natural range of walnut is from Vermont to the Great Plains and southward into Louisiana and Texas with most commercial production occurring in the central states. Heartwood is light gray brown to dark purple brown; sapwood is nearly white. The grain has exceptional natural beauty ranging from straight stripe to decorative swirl. The figure and texture can be altered by using different sawing methods. The variation of figures and textures allows walnut to be finished in a number of ways. Pores are large and quite visible. They can be filled for a smooth finish or left unfilled and open to create an Old English effect. Walnut is very strong, stable, moderately heavy, stiff, and has good shock resistance. It can be worked rather easily, has natural resistance to warping, shrinking, and decay, and is well suited to a wide range of finishes. Primary uses include solid wood, paneling and veneers, cabinets, furniture, gunstocks, and trim. *FINISH:* a natural finish (clear finish over bare wood) emphasizes the beauty of the grain and texture. Walnut bleaches well and can be highly stained. Walnut stain should only be used if a deep tone is desired. Rub to a high, lasting gloss.

Easy Softwood Identification Chart

Wood	Color Heartwood	Color Sapwood	Pattern Figure	Grain	Strength
Cedar	Reddish white	Creamy white	Distinct straight grain	Closed	Medium
Fir	Yellow	Creamy white	Resiny wild grain	Closed	Medium
Hemlock	Creamy brown	Slightly lighter	Coarse, uneven	Closed	Medium
Pine	Creamy red	Yellowish white	Straight, even	Closed	Medium
Redwood	Reddish brown	White	Straight, even	Closed	Good
Spruce	White	White	Fine, straight	Closed	Medium

Popular Softwoods

Cedar Largest production in southeastern and south-central states but common to entire eastern half of the United States. Heartwood is bright or dull red with light creamy-colored streaks running throughout; thin sapwood is nearly white. Knotty pattern and other markings are usually evident in straight grain. Cedar is not particularly strong but is very decay-resistant and cuts easily and cleanly. Stable in use and highly aromatic. Cedar is used in outdoor projects, chests, closet and sauna linings, bathroom paneling, and woodenware. *FINISH:* leave unfinished or apply clear finish over bare wood.

Fir Grows well in the Pacific and Rocky Mountain states. Heartwood is yellow; sapwood is creamy white. Wood is moderately heavy, hard, and stiff. Resin and grain patterns make fir a difficult wood to finish. Primary uses are in plywood, crates, and hidden areas of furniture. Makes a good plywood for cabinets and bookshelves. *FINISH:* a clear finish can be applied directly over the bare wood. Popular light and dark stains can be used after a coat of sealer has been applied. Enamel paints also work well.

Hemlock Species are found throughout the United States. Western hemlock is common in the Pacific Northwest and eastern hemlock is found in New England and the Great Lakes region. Heartwood and sapwood is creamy brown with a reddish purple tint. It is hard to distinguish sapwood from heartwood. Wood is coarse and uneven in texture. Hemlock is used in lumber, plywood, and pulpwood but is not very suitable to finishing.

Pine There are many species of pine distributed throughout the entire United States, but the major species used in furniture and cabinet construction are northern white, ponderosa, and yellow. White pine heartwood is creamy to light reddish brown, darkening with exposure; sapwood is yellowish white. Ponderosa and yellow are only slightly darker in color. Pine is moderately soft, light, stiff, and offers fair shock resistance. It is quite stable if seasoned properly but is somewhat susceptible to humidity and temperature changes. It has uniform texture and straight, even grain with small, barely visible pores. Some types of pine have numerous resinous deposits and knots that can give a rustic appearance. Pine is used in lumber, plywood, pulpwood, doors, trim, paneling, furniture, and cabinetry. The texture and figure enable a fine smooth finish to be applied without using fillers. It is soft wood, too soft for many furniture uses, but this is overcome by using hardwood veneers on framework constructed of pine. *FINISH:* can have a natural finish or can be stained in a variety of shades. Pine also accepts enamel paints well.

Redwood Limited to the West Coast from northern California to Washington. Heartwood varies from light cherry to dark reddish brown with obvious alternating summer and spring growth rings. Narrow sapwood is nearly white. Wood has even straight grain, is nonresinous, light in weight, and has an extremely high resistance to decay and insects. The wood is strong but is soft and somewhat brittle. Lacks interesting figure and is only marginally shock resistant. Redwood dries well, and when properly dried, is stable in use. It is a very desirable and popular wood used in siding, doors, paneling, planks, saunas, plywood, cooperage, fencing, furniture, decks, and many other outdoor uses. *FINISH:* apply clear finish to bare wood. Difficult to stain in lighter shades or as imitation of more expensive hardwood. Can be painted with enamels.

Spruce There are many species of spruce found throughout the entire United States. Heartwood is nearly white with slight red tinge. There is very little distinction between sapwood and heartwood. Spruce is generally straight grained with fine, uniform texture, only moderately strong for light weight, and dries easily with good stability. Primary uses include dimension lumber, plywood, paneling, furniture, millwork, musical instruments, boxes, and crates. *FINISH:* apply clear finish over bare wood or stain with light-colored stains.

Wood Construction

After you have determined the intended use of a wood product, have identified the type of wood that can best serve the intended use, have visualized how you want the piece to look when finished, and have decided on a budget, there is one more important consideration to make. Before buying and finishing any wood product—whether new, used, antique, or unfinished—consider the construction of the piece.

It is possible that the type of construction may not allow finishing or refinishing. Because of recent advancements in printing technology, many manufacturers can print reproductions of hardwood grain patterns and finishes on plastics. These plastic reproductions can then be laminated to plywood or particle board. Although relatively inexpensive, furniture constructed in this manner can only imitate appearance. Duplication of the warmth, quality, and the natural beauty of grain texture of genuine hardwood is impossible. If laminated furniture best fits your budget, do not expect to change finishes. It cannot be done.

There are four basic types of wood construction. Each has its own set of advantages. Selection depends on what best meets your specific needs, desires, and budget.

- **Wood Veneer Construction** From the least expensive wood products to the most expensive, plywood veneering is used in most furniture and cabinet construction. Plywood veneer consists of layers of wood glued to both sides of a center core. The core is generally a strong but inexpensive wood like chestnut. Sheets of wood, or veneers, are glued to the core with strong synthetic adhesives. The top or face layer is the best surface and is usually fine hardwood veneer, such as mahogany, birch, or walnut. The grain pattern of each layer is glued at right angles to the grain pattern of the next layer to provide the plywood with uniform strength in all directions. Wood shrinks and swells with temperature and humidity changes, but this gluing process ensures stability even under extreme conditions. Warpage and shrinkage are reduced to a minimum.

  Veneer originally was frowned upon because the adhesive properties of the older glues would not withstand unstable weather conditions. The glues used today, however, are extremely moisture resistant and fully waterproof. Plywood construction has advanced greatly during the past 25 years and is now recommended in many cases instead of solid wood.

  Quality wood veneer plywood may have veneer slices cut from the same log that will match when fitted together and glued in the same sequence in which they were cut. By arranging the slices in this manner, the final veneer will most effectively display the natural beauty of the true wood figure. As mentioned previously, the way in which a log is cut can change the grain pattern. Veneers can take advantage of the most distinguishing grain patterns because cuts can be thinner, making more cutting options available.

  Plywood veneers can be inlaid, permitting expensive exotic woods, such as ebony, teak, and rosewood, to be practically and economically incorporated into furniture design. The beauty of fine wood can be used to maximum effect to create unique, distinctive grain patterns.

  Weaker woods with excellent figure and color that are not suitable for solid wood construction can be incorporated into furniture design if used as veneers with stronger woods. Designs with curved forms are easier and less expensive to construct with veneers.

- **Solid Wood Construction** The one primary advantage solid wood construction has over quality veneer construction is the reduced likelihood that surface damage may occur. Solid wood construction has no veneer layers, eliminating the

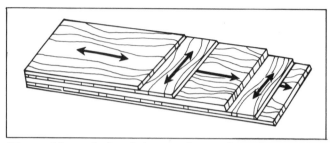

Plywood is made by gluing one layer of wood to another with grain patterns at right angles to each other.

chance of separating or chipping. Solid wood furniture and cabinets can usually be repaired and refinished easier because the grain is the same throughout the piece.

Wood expands and contracts with changes in temperature and humidity. Most of this movement is across the width of the surface, so a large, wide surface may split or warp during weather fluctuations. To control this dimensional stress, solid wood construction panels consist of narrow solid wood planks, permanently bonded together with adhesive, laid side-by-side to the appropriate width.

Whether the construction is solid or veneered, be certain that the frame is solid wood.

- **All Wood Construction** When construction is called all wood, this indicates that all exposed wood surfaces are wood throughout. Many inexpensive pieces utilize hollow sections in the construction to reduce costs and overall weight. Lift a corner or end of the piece to make sure it is heavy. Then knock on various exposed surfaces to be sure they do not sound hollow.

- **Other Construction Methods** These methods involve combining various materials in the construction. More than one type of wood, wood and metal, wood and plastic and particle board, and many other combinations can be used. Plastics, metals, and synthetic materials do not have the appeal of real wood, but their price generally makes them more affordable.

The Finishing Process

Regardless of the type of finish desired, whether stain, varnish, shellac, or lacquer, the basic procedure is practically the same. Each type of finish discussed follows this basic procedure; however, actual techniques, materials, and equipment for each finish do differ. Each operation is in easy-to-follow steps. All materials and equipment are readily available at most paint and hardware stores. These are the basic steps in the finishing process.

Preparing the Surface Whether the wood you plan to finish is unfinished or has a finish coat on it, the surface must be properly prepared to accept the new finish. A poorly prepared surface will result in a disappointing final product. The existing finish must be thoroughly removed, any defects or damages must be repaired or minimized, the surface must be sanded and smoothed with the appropriate abrasive, and the smoothed surface must be cleaned and washed.

Obtaining the Proper Color The wood may be the perfect color or too light or too dark. Depending on your needs and desires, color can be altered according-ly. If the wood lacks natural color or if you want the wood to appear darker or imitate another type of wood, stain can be applied to the prepared, raw surface to change the original color. If the natural wood is too dark for your purposes, bleach can be used to lighten the color. If the wood is the desired color in the raw state, you can move directly to the next step.

Filling Wood Pores All wood has pores, but some species have more prominent pores than others. If a smooth finish is desired, these pores must be filled, after the surface is stained or bleached, with a paste or liquid filler. Some furniture designs are noted for their rough, open-grained appearance. These designs and other types of woods do not require fillers. Some fillers act as sealers to provide a good base for the final finish; others require an additional sealer coat.

Applying the Final Finish The raw wood surface has now been stained and filled, if desired, and is ready for a transparent protective topcoat. This topcoat can be shellac, varnish, lacquer, oil, or paste wax, depending on the intended use of the wood product. Several coats are often required. The topcoat has two primary purposes: to protect the surface and enhance the appearance. The advantages and proper application techniques for each type of finish will be discussed in later chapters.

Smoothing and Rubbing The transparent finish coat must be polished with a light abrasive to remove brush marks, dust, and other surface imperfections. This is a tiring, time-consuming process but essential to a professional-looking smooth finish. Several materials can be used for smoothing the topcoat.

There are many new, easy-to-use materials on the market to simplify these five steps of the basic finishing procedure. These new materials are also dur-able and easy to maintain. The methods and tech-niques for applying each type of finish, presented in the following chapters, incorporate the use of these labor-saving materials. Even inexperienced handy-men can know the satisfaction of creating a beautiful wood finish.

Wood Finishing Chart

WOOD	STAIN		FILLER		PAINT	BLEACH	NATURAL
	TYPE	COLOR	MIX	COLOR			
HARDWOODS							
Ash	Any	Any	Heavy	White to brown	Yes	Easy	Yes
Aspen	Water	Amber, light tones	None	None	Yes	None	Yes
Basswood	Water	Reddish brown tones	None	None	Yes	None	No
Beech	Water	Reddish brown maple	Thin	Red to brown	Yes	Easy	No
Birch	Any	Maple, walnut, mahogany	Thin	Natural to brown	Yes	Easy	Yes
Butternut	Water	Walnut, oak	Medium	Light brown	No	Easy	Yes
Cherry	Water	Red to brown	Thin	Brown, red, black	No	Difficult	Yes
Chestnut	Oil	Red to brown	Heavy	Red to brown	Yes	Difficult	Yes
Ebony	Water	Reddish brown	None	None	No	None	Yes
Elm	Water	Light red to brown	Heavy	Dark brown tones	Yes	Difficult	Yes
Gum	Any	Maple, walnut	Thin	Match wood	Yes	Easy	Yes
Hickory	Water	Red to brown	Heavy	Brown tones	No	Easy	Yes
Mahogany	Water	Reddish brown tones	Medium	Red, black, brown	No	Easy	Yes
Maple	Oil/Water	Maple	Thin or none	Natural	Yes	Easy	Yes
Oak	Water	Greenish brown tones	Heavy	Brown tones	No	Easy	Yes
Poplar	Oil/Water	Red to brown	None	None	Yes	None	No
Rosewood	Water	Reddish tones	Medium	Dark red to black	No	Difficult	Yes
Sycamore	Water	Amber or brown	Thin	Light brown tones	Yes	Easy	Yes
Teak	Oil/Water	Brown tones	Heavy	Natural or brown	No	Easy	Yes
Walnut	Water	Walnut, maple, oak	Medium	Brown to black	No	Easy	Yes
SOFTWOODS							
Cedar	None	None	None	None	No	Difficult	Yes
Fir	Oil	Brown tones	None	None	Yes	None	No
Hemlock	Oil/Water	Red to brown	None	None	Yes	None	No
Pine	Oil/Water	Brown tones	None	None	Yes	None	Yes
Redwood	Oil	Reddish tones	None	None	Yes	Difficult	Yes
Spruce	Oil/Water	Amber or brown	None	None	Yes	None	No

Removing the Old Finish

If you have purchased an unfinished wood product or have constructed a project from raw wood, you can turn to the next chapter on preparing the raw wood surface for finishing. If, however, you have a favorite piece of furniture or have purchased one second-hand that is in obvious need of a new finish, the existing finish must be stripped first.

It is not always necessary to remove an existing finish, nor is it advisable to remove a finish from beautifully aged wood that has developed a rich patina. Stripping can lessen the value of an antique by destroying the warmth and mellow tones that natural aging has created. In this case the finish should be restored.

Many times though, the original finish has been damaged beyond restoration. Scratches, gouges, and areas of discoloration detract from the beauty and reduce the ability of a finish to protect the wood. If you suspect the finish condition is too poor to restore, simply draw the bowl of a spoon across the finished surface, preferably in a hidden area. If the finish flakes off easily, refinishing is necessary. Sometimes, the wood's natural beauty has been hidden under multiple coats of paint. If this is the case, the paint must be totally removed.

When it becomes apparent that finish removal is necessary, you must determine which method of stripping will ensure the most satisfactory results without damaging the wood surface. Refinishing wood yourself allows you to have total control over the quality of the job and the overall beauty of the piece.

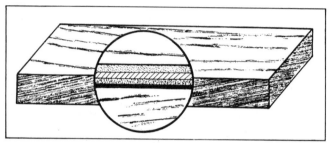

The four layers of finish include (from top to bottom): coat of hard paste wax, clear finish, sealer, and a stain.

The Existing Finish

Stripping is the process of removing an existing finish to reveal the raw wood surface. Before sanding or applying a chemical solvent to the finish, identify the finish to determine exactly what to do. The last chapter explains how to do this. A finish generally consists of several layers of different materials. The succession of layers from top to bottom is usually a combination of the following: a wax or polish topcoat; one or several layers of clear or colored finish material, either shellac, lacquer, or varnish; a coat of shellac or sealer to provide a base for the finish; and a colored stain that penetrates and gives color to the raw wood surface.

Consider these layers when planning the stripping operation. Determine which layers are damaged. If the color is acceptable, is it in the stain or one of the finish coats? If scratches and discolored areas mar the finish layers, only these have to be removed. If the original color is achieved through a stain and not one of the finish layers, the color can be saved and restaining avoided. This is particularly desirable if the wood has developed a beautiful, rich patina. Only a new finish will have to be applied. If, however, all layers are damaged or the color is in one of the finish coats or the color is unacceptable, stripping to the raw wood surface will be necessary as all layers will have to be replaced.

The above finish appears to need complete removal.

The spoon test indicates that the finish is very brittle.

Once you determine exactly which layers must be removed, you can select the proper stripping method and appropriate materials that will remove only the layers you want to remove.

Stripping Methods

There are three basic finish-removing methods, each differing in difficulty, time, and expense:

- Chemical Paint Removers: These are available in several forms, with liquid and paste being the most widely used. There is no difference between paint removers and varnish removers; either product will strip paint or finish materials. These solvents loosen the existing finish so it can be lifted off with light scraping either with a putty knife or steel wool.
- Mechanical Removal: Finish can be removed by hand scraping, hand sanding, power sanding, or with a combination of these.
- Heat: The old finish can be softened by the heat of a blowtorch or electric heating tool and then can be scraped off gently.

Chemical Removers Paint and varnish removers are more expensive and messier than the other methods, but they are far superior because they offer the novice greater control over the stripping process by reducing the chances of making a mistake or damaging the wood surface. Chemical paint removers generally remove just the finish layers, leaving the original stain intact. They will not harm patina, delicate surface carvings, or the original wood surface. Paint removers, because they do not generally contain water, will not damage glue, raise the grain, or loosen veneer surfaces.

The consistency of paint removers ranges from a thin liquid to a heavy paste. Liquids are less expensive, but the heavy pastes are more efficient. Paste removers do not run or drip from vertical surfaces and do not evaporate as quickly as liquids. The longer a remover remains in contact with the finish, the more thoroughly it will soften the finish. Several applications may be required when thin solvents are used to strip multilayer finishes, particularly on vertical surfaces.

Cost should not be the primary concern in selecting a paint remover. The retail price you pay is determined primarily by the chemical content. All removers will soften the paint or varnish, but the less expensive varieties may leave residues that are hard to remove. If not removed properly and completely, these residues can hamper the ability of new finishing materials to adhere to the stripped surface. Should this happen, the entire finishing process will have to be redone.

These residues are usually waxlike compounds. (Removers contain wax to retard evaporation, keeping the remover moist and active for a longer time.) This wax can become imbedded in the pores of the wood. Cheaper removers contain inexpensive waxes that must be washed from the wood surface with turpentine or paint thinner. Even removers labeled "no cleanup" may leave a minimal amount of residue; therefore the surface should still be wiped with paint thinner or alcohol. Sanding will also help remove residue.

The most expensive removers may be labeled "water-wash." These removers are formulated with emulsifiers which allow the chemicals and waxes to mix freely with water and rinse away easily. After the finish has been thoroughly softened by the remover, everything can be stripped by scrubbing the surface with steel wool or a cloth that has been dipped in water. The wood can even be rinsed with a garden hose if extreme care and the necessary precautions are taken. Many older pieces of furniture, however, may have water soluble glues as part of their construction. Should these glues become wet, their bonding power will be destroyed. Never use water on veneers. The moisture can cause the veneer to wrinkle or loosen.

Another important factor to consider when selecting a paint remover is flammability. Many paint removers, particularly the less expensive ones, are highly flammable, which increases the hazard of fire. These removers must be used with extreme caution, especially when working indoors. More expensive removers contain chemicals which help prevent the other chemicals from burning. These removers are labeled "nonflammable" and should be used when working indoors or in a confined area.

All factors considered, the more expensive paint or varnish removers are probably more economical in the long run. They do a faster and more efficient job, they require less clean-up time, and they are safer to use. They use better chemicals that thoroughly remove the finish, revealing a clean raw wood surface.

Mechanical Removal Removing a finish by scraping and sanding is less expensive than stripping with a paint remover. Mechanical removal also creates very little mess—the sawdust-type residue can be vacuumed up quite easily. It is also a relatively quick process. The drawbacks of sanding and scraping, however, can be considerable. Many professionals recommend that novice handymen stay away from this process entirely.

Sanding is effective, but it is impossible to remove the existing finish without removing some of the wood. Power sanding will remove considerably more wood than hand sanding. Removing a thin layer of wood will not harm the surface unless the wood has had the time to develop patina. This impressive quality should be saved whenever possible because it increases the value and beauty of older furniture. It is hard to retain patina when sanding. If any of it is accidently removed, all of it must be sanded off to provide a uniform surface color.

If the wood you plan to refinish is not old enough to have developed patina, sanding can be used to remove the finish. If, however, the piece has delicate carvings or moldings, sanding can damage these surfaces because finish removal requires a heavy open-coat sandpaper (explained in the next chapter) and a heavy hand. Less coarse abrasives may be used, but then finish removal becomes a tedious, time-consuming project. Even on large flat surfaces, sanding and scraping can cause rounded corners or damage by cutting too deeply into the surface. It is relatively easy for the beginner to gouge a surface with a scraper.

Because high-quality hardwoods are becoming more scarce, wood veneers are being used more in furniture construction. Often the distinctive wood grain pattern that gives a veneer its beauty is only a fraction of an inch thick. This pattern can easily be destroyed by sanding. Only use chemical removers and steel wool on veneer surfaces.

Heat Although an electric-element heater may effectively remove finish or paint from large flat surfaces, such as the sides of a house, it has little use as a finish remover to the home handyman. The process is much slower than the other methods, generally leaves a residue that must be removed with a chemical solvent, and presents a fire hazard or, at minimum, a chance of scorching the wood surface. This technique will not be discussed in detail.

How to Use Paint Remover

Stripping a finish with a chemical remover cannot be done without making a mess—accept this fact and prepare yourself and your work area. Cover your work area with newspapers or cardboard. Some chemicals can dissolve plastic so avoid using this material. Wear old clothes and shoes.

Safety First The handling of potentially dangerous chemicals requires certain safeguards. All chemical paint removers contain strong chemicals that can injure you. To avoid an accident follow these safety rules carefully:

- Wear rubber gloves and a long-sleeved shirt to protect your skin from chemicals which can burn or cause irritation.
- Wear safety goggles to protect your eyes from accidental splashing.
- Work in a well-ventilated area. If you cannot work outdoors, choose an area that offers good ventilation. Never work in closed, confined areas. Most paint removers are highly flammable with low flash points. Fumes, should they come in contact with flame, can ignite suddenly, causing an explosion. Do not use near an open flame, pilot light, lighted cigarette, or any device that may cause sparks. Never smoke when using these

chemicals. These fumes can irritate eyes and can damage the membranes of your nose, mouth, throat, and lungs.
- Keep children away from your work area and refinishing materials. Most are highly toxic, caustic products.
- Do not store paint removers for extensive periods. Excessive pressure can develop inside the container causing it to rupture or the contents to spray out when the container is opened.
- Rags or brushes used for chemical finish removal should be destroyed or cleaned thoroughly and stored in a well-ventilated area.
- Always follow instructions and precautions printed on the remover container carefully.

Which Type of Remover? The chemical you use to remove a finish is determined by the type of finish. To strip a shellac finish, use denatured alcohol. Thorough removal may require several applications, particularly if there are multiple finish coats. Apply alcohol liberally with a brush and rub gently with steel wool. The same procedure should be used for lacquer finishes, except lacquer thinner should be used as the solvent instead of alcohol. Paint and varnish finishes can be removed with any of the commercial paint or varnish removers available at most paint and hardware stores. Follow all label instructions carefully.

Tools Assemble all the necessary tools at your work area before starting the stripping process. The basic stripping equipment should include:

- a high-quality paint or varnish remover that will effectively soften the finish
- denatured alcohol solvent
- gum turpentine or mineral spirits to remove waxy residues
- a wide round-cornered putty knife or wide putty knife
- used medium-sized bristle paintbrushes
- fairly fine steel wool pads (see next chapter)
- a variety of cloths in different sizes and textures
- an assortment of materials for cleaning hard-to-reach areas, such as cotton swabs, string or twine, an old toothbrush, and sticks
- plenty of newspapers and cardboard to collect dripping remover
- the necessary tools for removing hardware
- an assortment of covered containers for storage of solvents and used materials

Removing a Finish from a Wood Surface Before beginning the actual stripping process, all hardware, such as mirror supports, hinges, and handles, must be removed and cleaned separately. Plug all screw holes with paper wads. Glass and mirrors must be removed from their frames. All drawers should be removed and placed so drawer fronts are horizontal. After the hinges have been removed lay all doors flat.

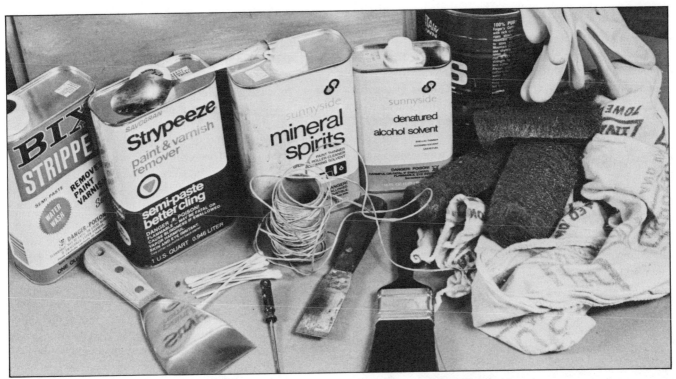

The tools and materials shown above are used in the removal of an existing finish.

Repair loose joints prior to stripping (see next chapter for repair technique).

To efficiently and thoroughly remove a finish from a wooden surface, follow these steps carefully:

1. Pour the remover into a clean empty container. The remover must be applied in sufficient quantity to permit the chemicals to soften the finish before they evaporate. Lay the chemical on thickly with an old paintbrush loaded to capacity. Do not brush back and forth. Excessive brushing causes evaporation and slows the chemical reaction. Concentrate on one small area at a time. If you try to cover an entire project, some areas may evaporate or completely dry.

2. If an area begins to appear dull or the remover appears thin in areas, lay on more remover. Keep the entire section you are working on wet. Never allow the remover to dry completely. The remover stays in place longer on horizontal surfaces. Vertical surfaces may require more applications. If the piece is small enough, turn it so each surface can be worked on horizontally.

3. Allow the chemicals to work approximately 20 minutes or until the paint or finish lifts from the surface. The remover needs time to work effectively. The surface will appear wrinkled or bubbly if the chemical reaction has taken place and the finish is softened to the raw wood.

4. If you are using a non-water soluble remover, carefully place the edge of the putty knife on the surface and gently scrape the softened finish

1. Apply a heavy coat of the chemical finish remover with an old paintbrush.

2. Allow the remover to remain on the surface until the finish seems dissolved.

from the wood surface in the direction of the grain. The corners of the putty knife are sharp, so it is easy to gouge or scratch the wood surface. Apply light, even pressure. Some refinishers file the corners of the putty knife round to help prevent gouging the surface. Scrape the softened finish into a container or onto a piece of stiff cardboard. Clean the knife as necessary.

If you are using a water soluble remover and have adequately softened the finish, the excess can be hosed off with clean water, provided there are no delicate veneers or water soluble glues in the construction of the piece. If you plan to wash the piece outdoors with a garden hose, be aware that the chemicals used in the remover can damage or kill grass. Try to hose it off on a gravel surface. If the use of a hose is inconvenient, rinse the remover off with a clean sponge or rags and plenty of water. A nearby floor drain will facilitate cleanup.

5. For hard-to-reach areas that cannot be scraped, such as grooves, crevices, moldings, or intricate carvings, common household items can be used to remove the finish after it has been softened with a non-water soluble remover. Water soluble removers should rinse clean, but stubborn areas can be loosened with a pad of wet steel wool. Steel wool dipped in the remover can sometimes be used effectively. Heavy string, or twine, works well on narrow grooves or turned surfaces. A stiff toothbrush is excellent for grooves, fluting, and finely detailed carved designs. Cotton swabs or a sharp stick wrapped in

3. Scrape the dissolved finish into a container with either a pushing action or a pulling action.

5. Remover can be applied to small corners, grooves, and carvings with a cotton swab.

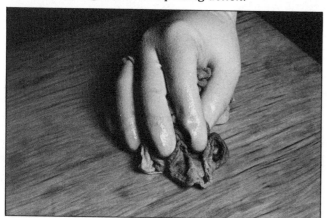

4. Water-wash removers can be rinsed with water.

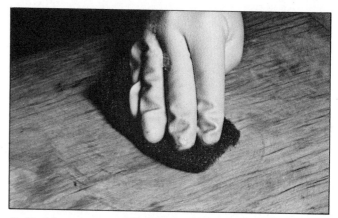

6. Stubborn areas of finish can be steel wooled.

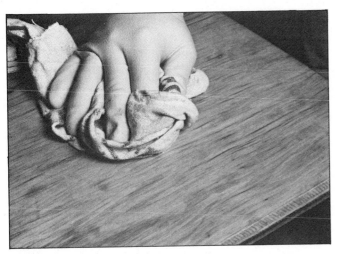

7. *Wipe surface with clean cloth.*

8. *Remaining spots of finish, like those on the chair spindle above, appear dark or glossy.*

9. *Apply additional remover to spot.*

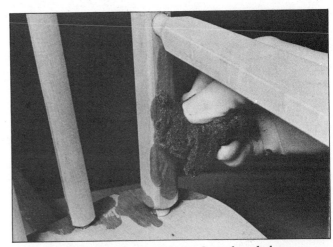

10. *Lightly rub the spot with steel wool and clean.*

cloth can be used on extremely narrow channels or grooves. Removing finish from these hard-to-reach surfaces requires more time, patience, and effort, but complete removal is equally as important as for large, highly visible flat surfaces.

Water soluble removers should rinse clean, but stubborn areas can be loosened with a pad of wet steel wool.

6. After most of the softened finish has been removed by scraping, wiping, or rinsing, wipe the entire surface section with a clean cloth to take off any remaining traces of softened finish.

7. If any of the old paint or finish is still visible in spots, apply the remover and allow to stand until the material lifts. This process can be speeded up by rubbing the area lightly with steel wool as more remover is applied. Remember the new finish will not adhere or dry properly on areas that are not completely stripped. On some pieces of very old furniture or cabinets, you may discover several thick coats of paint that will be difficult, if not impossible, to re-

move with this general procedure. Try laying down several coats of remover followed with a covering of wet burlap or cloth to minimize evaporation. Allow to stand several hours, checking occasionally to make sure the remover is not becoming too dry. Remove the softened finish with a putty knife.

8. If the piece you are refinishing is very large and your budget is limited, use an inexpensive remover to strip most of the finish. Then apply a thin coat of water soluble remover to clean up stubborn areas.

9. Many paint and varnish removers will leave the stain and wood filler intact. If this stain is not desired, it must be bleached or sanded from the surface (see the next chapter for proper bleaching and sanding techniques). Bleaching not only removes stain, it also lightens the natural color of the wood.

10. After the finish has been thoroughly removed and the piece has dried for a few hours, carefully examine all surfaces to be sure that there are no remaining patches of the old finish. These areas

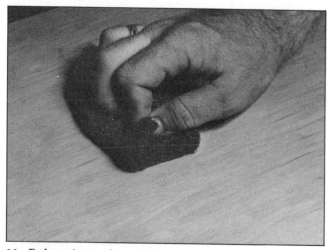

11. Rub entire surface with 2/0 steel wool.

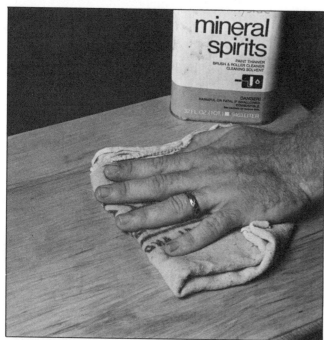

12. Wipe surface with mineral spirits.

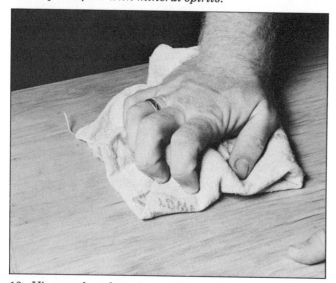

13. Vigorously rub surface with clean cloth.

appear as glossy or dark spots. Only bare wood should be visible.

11. Rub the surface gently with 2/0 steel wool or clean cloths soaked in denatured alcohol or mineral spirits to remove any waxy residues left by the chemical removers, particularly non-water soluble varieties. Go over the surface thoroughly. For small hard-to-reach areas use cotton swabs or cloth wrapped around sharp implements dipped in the same solvent.

12. Wipe thoroughly with clean cloths, exerting as much pressure as possible.

13. Allow to dry 24 hours.

14. Discard all used cloths, newspapers, and containers of the old finish in an outdoor trash can. Brushes used for paint-remover application should never be used for anything but paint remover. Clean the brush with mineral spirits.

With the old finish completely removed, you can now examine the raw wood surface to determine if there is damage in need of repair and also to determine the amount of final sanding required to achieve a smooth surface for finishing. Stripping is but the first step in proper surface preparation.

Problem Finishes Some of the newer finishes can be very difficult to remove. These tough finishes, such as urethanes, epoxies, and penetrating resins, penetrate wood deeply, giving the surface a hard plastic

14. The stripped wood is ready for refinishing.

texture. They are durable and seldom require removing. If they must be removed, most chemical removers will not be effective, and mechanical removal would remove too much of the wood. Heat may be the only method of removal that will work, but extreme care must be used because the electric heating element can cause a fire. The best solution is to apply a coat of the existing finish.

Removing the Finish Mechanically

Many times an old varnish finish will be so brittle that the varnish actually flakes off under the even pressure of a steel hand scraper. Be cautious not to gouge or damage the wood surface with the corners of the scraper. Hook-type scrapers are available for reaching corners and other areas that are hard to reach.

Hold the scraper at a 90-degree angle to the surface with both hands. The thumbs should be positioned behind the scraper and used to push the scraper forward in the direction of the grain. Change the cutting angle periodically to achieve uniform scraping action. Always scrape in the direction of the grain. Scrape until bare wood is revealed. Sand thoroughly.

Hand sanding can be used to remove a finish, but this is generally a very tedious task. Sanding techniques and the various abrasive papers are covered in detail in the next chapter. For stripping, the following procedure is recommended:

1. Select an abrasive paper that is somewhere between coarse and medium, about No. 80, and that will efficiently take off the finish without removing too much wood.

2. Sand only in the direction of the grain, applying even pressure. A sanding block will allow you to apply more pressure, more evenly on large flat surfaces. Replace the abrasive paper as it becomes worn.

3. Remove as much of the finish as possible with this coarse paper. As the bare wood begins to show through, change to a finer grade of paper, such as No. 120. Sand until only bare wood is visible and begin the smoothing process detailed in the next chapter.

Preparing the Surface for Finishing

The quality of the final finish depends directly on the care and workmanship devoted to surface preparation. The importance of this step cannot be overemphasized. The final finish coat will not conceal any surface imperfections and damages. In fact, defects which may be barely visible on a raw wood surface, will be magnified beneath a transparent finish. These conspicuous blemishes lower the value of the time, effort and materials that went into creating the piece. Close attention to detail, time, and patience are essential to properly preparing wood for finishing or refinishing.

Repairing a Wood Surface

All woods are susceptible to damages and aging. Even the strongest and hardest hardwoods may dent, gouge, scratch, split, or warp when subjected to the stress of daily use and changing weather conditions. These imperfections must be detected and repaired before starting the finishing process. It is much easier to repair damaged wood while it is in the unfinished state than to try to repair after finishing.

Thoroughly examine all raw wood surfaces before starting any work. Even a new unfinished wood product directly off a showroom floor can have hammer dents, cracks, and scratches. If the wood is presently finished, the existing finish or paint must first be removed to determine the true extent of the damage and to discover any previously hidden imperfections. Even the slightest imperfection should be repaired before moving on. Most repairs require additional sanding and smoothing, so it is best to make all necessary repairs after stripping and before sanding.

Novices are most likely to encounter simple surface repairs which can be repaired relatively easily. Major furniture repairs often require special tools and techniques beyond the experience of most occasional wood finishers and refinishers. Therefore, major repairs are not covered in this book. Refer to the Basic Wood Repair Guide for information on how to quickly repair common damage.

Basic Wood Repair Guide

Scratches
- Scratches along the grain are harder to see.
- Most small surface scratches can be removed by light sanding.
- Never sandpaper just the scratch; sand the surrounding area as well to prevent removing too much wood from one area.
- Moderately deep scratches can be removed with a scraper followed by sanding. Use great care not to scrape too deep, particularly on veneered wood.
- Never plane a surface ready for finishing.

Gouges
- Gouges and severe scratches are generally too deep for sanding and must be filled with a patching compound.
- Several products can be used as fillers. Wood-patching compounds are available in several colors. These compounds differ in their ability to accept stain. Some are absorbent and will accept stain easily; others will not. Some shrink as they dry, and others have less tendency to shrink. The common compounds are:
  Plastic Water Putty—Inexpensive but effective putty is packaged in powder form; light cream color, sets quickly, and cannot be remixed. Apply with putty knife, wipe off excess, allow to dry thoroughly, and sand until smooth. Dry, powdered colors can be added to change color.
  Wood Compound Paste—Hard paste form is available in many common wood colors. No mixing. Work desired amount into gouge with putty knife, allow to dry one hour, and sand well.
  Plastic Wood—Application is easy, dries quickly, and is available in many colors. Work into gouge with knife, dry for about fifteen minutes, and sand until smooth. Deeper gouges may require two layers. Does not absorb stain well.
  Putty—Avoid oil-based putty because it requires a lengthy drying period. A simple, effective putty can be made by mixing heated animal glue with sawdust, preferably of the same wood that is being repaired. Work mixture into gouge, allow to dry two hours, and sand until smooth. Very inexpensive.

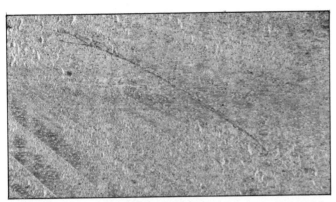

1. Scratches on raw wood are common.

2. Remove scratch by sanding.

1. Gouges and nicks must be filled.

2. Apply wood filler with putty knife.

3. Sand dried filler level with surface.

Cracks	• As wood ages and dries out, cracks may occur.
	• Severe cracks require replacement of the damaged part(s).
	• Simple cracks with the grain are usually clean and can be glued with epoxy cement and clamped securely. Never use glue without clamps.
	• Dowels can be used to increase stability and strength of load-bearing parts.
	• Cracks across the grain are often very irregular and may require complete replacement. Try glue first and, if possible, add a supporting splint in a hidden area.
	• End-grain cracks may be filled with patching compound. Sand when completely dry. Use a nonshrinking compound if possible.
Dents	• High-use areas of wooden products are susceptible to dents.
	• If a dent or hammer mark is shallow, the compressed wood fibers may be returned to their original condition by wetting the area to make the fibers swell.
	• If the dent does not return to its original condition, place several thicknesses of a moistened cloth over the dent and press on it with a hot clothes iron. Repeat several times if necessary.
	• Sand until smooth.
Nicks	• Small nicks may resemble dents, but nicks generally have some wood loss.
	• Nicks can be filled with any patching compound, but these compounds have

1. Wood often cracks as it ages.

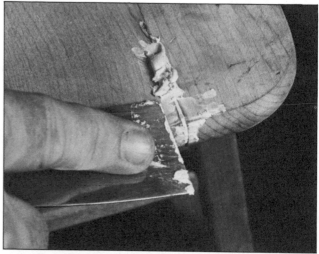

2. Fill crack with wood putty.

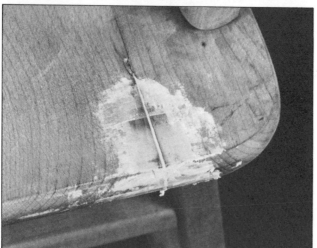

3. Two or three layers may be needed.

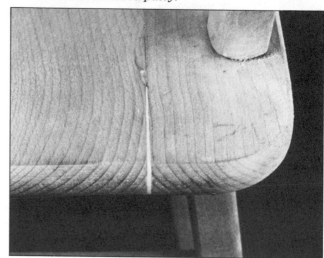

4. Sand thoroughly when dry.

varying degrees of absorption and some may stain better than others. Try blending the filler into the surrounding wood by selecting a color closest to that of the intended finish.

- Large, deep nicks may require several layers of patching compound.
- Sand until smooth.

Exposed Nailheads

- Drive raised heads below wood surface with nail set.
- Fill hole with patching compound, allow to dry, and sand until smooth.
- Screw heads can be treated in the same manner.
- A more professional way to conceal screw heads is to fill the hole with a wooden plug. Wooden plugs are available in many common hardwoods and softwoods, making a close match relatively easy to accomplish. Plugs can also be cut from scraps of similar wood with a plug-cutter drill bit or can be cut from a wooden dowel of appropriate size.

Loose Joints

- Clean out joint thoroughly.
- Fill joint with patching compound, allow to dry, and trim excess with a razor blade.
- If joint is relatively simple, white glue can be used to tighten the joint slightly.
- The greater the problem, the stronger the glue should be.
- Several wood-swelling products are available that may tighten only slightly loose joints.

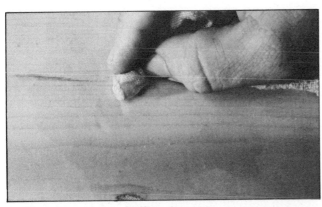

1. Water may raise shallow dents.

1. Countersink protruding nailheads.

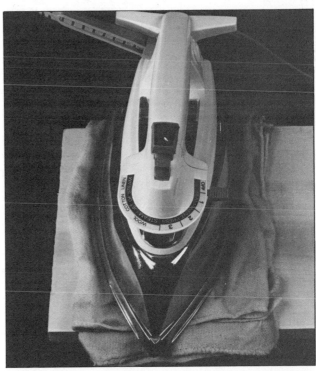

2. Place a damp cloth over deeper dents. Apply a hot iron. Repeat as necessary.

2. Apply wood putty to holes.

3. Smooth putty with screwdriver.

4. Sand with 100 grit sandpaper.

5. Sand with 220 grit sandpaper.

Warping
- If moisture content changes, wood will warp.
- Warp may be minimized or improved by wetting the concave side and clamping flat. Clamping may require weeks or months depending on the severity of the warp. Do not clamp tight. Extreme pressure may crack the wood.
- Allow wood to dry thoroughly, sand, and finish on both sides.

Burns
- Scrape all charred areas with a scraper, putty knife, or knife.
- If the damaged area is shallow, sand, and blend into surrounding surface area.
- If the depression made by scraping is noticeable but rather small, a wood filler can be used to raise the damaged surface.
- If the burn is extensive, the entire damaged area must be removed and replaced with a patch of wood with color and grain pattern that will match the surrounding surface.
- Patches should be cigar-shaped or trapezoid-shaped to help hide borders.
- A tight fit is essential to success. Pronounced borders will result from an improperly fitting patch. Use extreme care in drawing the template and cutting the patch, to ensure a proper fit.
- Glue in patch, fill cracks, and sand thoroughly.

Missing Wood
- Chipped surfaces or broken corners can be repaired if the damage is not too severe.
- For damaged corners or edges, the area can be built up with patching compound.
- Roughen the exposed edges and surface of minor chips and fill with patching compound. Rough edges will increase the strength of the bond.
- For more severe chips, roughen the damaged area, and drive several staples or small brads into the area but below the finished surface of the repair to increase the strength.
- Press several layers of patching compound over the area. Allow each layer to dry thoroughly before adding another layer.
- Sand new surface thoroughly until smooth.

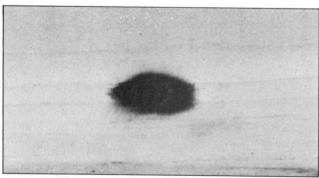

1. Shallow burns can be repaired.

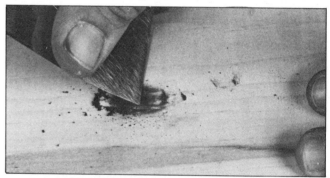

2. Scrape out all charred areas.

3. Apply wood putty to damaged area.

4. Sand level with surrounding surface.

1. *Severe chips can be repaired.*

2. *Roughen edges of damaged area.*

3. *Nail several small brads into chip.*

4. *Apply wood putty.*

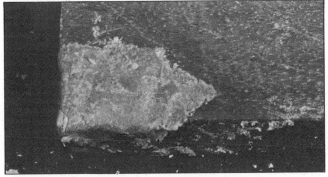

5. *Form corner with fingers or framework.*

6. *Sand thoroughly when dry.*

Veneer Repair	• Veneered furniture is more susceptible to damage than solid wood, but small repairs are not difficult to make.

• Veneered furniture is more susceptible to damage than solid wood, but small repairs are not difficult to make.

• Small imperfections such as dents, scratches, and bruises can be repaired by the same methods used for solid wood.

• Veneered edges can lift away from the other edges. Scrape out old glue and dirt carefully. Apply glue to wood surface and press veneer into glue. Squeeze out excess glue and wipe with damp cloth. Clamp veneer to core stock.

• Blisters or waves are caused by excess moisture. They can be repaired a number of ways depending on severity of damage. For blisters with an unbroken surface, place a moderately heated clothes iron over the blister. The iron removes moisture and softens the existing glue. For large unbroken blisters, make a slit through the blister with a sharp knife. Work glue beneath the blister and apply clamps until the glue hardens completely. If the blister is cracked and dirt has

worked its way beneath the veneer, make a cut in the shape of an X. Lift each section and clean thoroughly. Glue, clamp, and allow to completely harden.
- Missing veneer must be replaced with an inlay of the same thickness, color, and grain pattern. Trim damaged area, carefully draw a template, trim inlay accurately, glue, and clamp. Patching veneer may be available from a specialized lumber dealer.
- Rough edges should be filled and sanded to provide a smooth surface for finishing.

Sanding for Smoothness

With the old finish completely removed and all necessary surface repairs made, the raw wood surface must now be cleaned and smoothed to a fine uniform condition that will evenly accept finishing materials and, ultimately, enhance the grain pattern. The surface must be totally free from roughness, dirt, chemical remover residue, or any foreign matter or the final reflective finish will highlight only the problem areas.

Don't trust sight alone. Even clean, smooth-looking areas can harbor dried chemical removers, waxy deposit residues, and dirt that will interfere with certain finish properties, such as ease of application, adhesion, drying time, and uniformity of color. Even newly purchased unfinished furniture is not exempt from this important sanding step.

Sanding requires more care when refinishing older wood than it does when preparing to finish new wood. Older wood has a highly desirable and beautiful character called patina—the soft, mellow appearance wood acquires through aging. As wood ages, it darkens in a special way, acquiring a particular quality and character that is virtually impossible to duplicate by finishing. Extensive sanding or use of the wrong abrasive can destroy patina, reducing the beauty and overall value of an older piece. New wood has not had time to develop patina; therefore, the only concern is achieving a satin-smooth surface.

Proper surface preparation and smoothing requires time, effort, patience, a thorough awareness of the types of abrasives which can be used for specific jobs, and employing the proper sanding technique. Sandpaper tends to be overused. When only light sanding is required, steel wool is a better choice. The degree of smoothness required depends on the product, its intended use, and the type of wood. A rustic pine bench does not require as fine a surface as a mahogany dresser. Knowing what type of abrasive to use, where to use it, and how to use it are essential to creating a professional-looking finish. The following section describes the various abrasives used in wood finishing and provides the basic instructions for their proper use.

Sandpaper

Sandpaper derived its name many years ago when heavy papers were actually coated with sand. As technologies for abrasive production advanced, several minerals were found to be more suitable for abrasive papers. Today, four important minerals are used in the manufacture of sandpapers commonly used in wood refinishing. They are flint, garnet, aluminum oxide, and silicon carbide. Emery cloth is a popular abrasive, but it is more suitable to metal polishing so it is not included in this discussion.

Flint Paper The abrasive in this paper is quartz or silica that is mined from natural mineral deposits. The coating has a yellowish, off-white color. Flint paper is the most common abrasive found in hardware stores, lumberyards, and home improvement centers because it is inexpensive. The glue used to fasten the grit to the backing is cheap, and the backing is often inferior to other abrasive papers.

Although economical, flint paper is not recommended for wood refinishing because it wears out very fast. The quartz grit loses its cutting edge more quickly than other abrasives and must be replaced often, making flint paper less of a bargain than it initially appears to be. It is hard to achieve the same smoothness with flint paper that is possible with higher quality abrasives.

Flint papers are suitable for finish removing because the old finish will clog the coating of any abrasive paper very quickly. Here the least expensive sandpaper is the most economical. Flint papers are available in a wide range of grades and grits.

Garnet Paper This abrasive paper has a reddish brown mineral coating and a hard, sharp texture. It is widely used in both professional and industrial wood refinishing. Garnet papers have gained in popularity in recent years because they are durable, strong, have good cutting ability, and are probably more economical than the less expensive flint paper in the long run. As the garnet grit wears, it fractures irregularly, creating more sharp cutting edges, so the paper continues to cut sharply and uniformly.

The above abrasives are (from left to right): fine emery cloth, extra coarse flint (40 grit), coarse garnet (60), medium flint (100), fine garnet (150), extra fine flint (220), extra fine silicone carbide (320), and superfine silicone carbide (400).

Many professional wood refinishers prefer garnet papers for fine sanding on raw wood or final finishes because it cuts fast and evenly, creating a fine, smooth surface. Garnet paper will dull quickly when used on metal surfaces.

The paper is available in many grades and grits making it suitable for most refinishing steps. Try both flint and garnet papers. The advantages of garnet papers are quite noticeable.

Aluminum Oxide Paper This synthetic abrasive is created by processing the mineral bauxite at extremely high temperatures in an electric furnace. The resulting uniform grayish brown abrasive is versatile, sharp, tough, and wears very well.

Aluminum oxide papers are used extensively for both hand and power sanding. This abrasive is particularly well suited to smoothing final varnish, shellac, or lacquer finishes because of its fast cutting action. Coarseness ranges from very fine to medium coarse.

Silicone Carbide Paper This is another synthetic abrasive, created by fusing silica sand and coke. The black crystalline abrasive usually has a waterproof backing making it an excellent paper for wet sanding, which is quicker and easier than dry sanding. The grit is extremely hard, sharp, and irregular, assuring superior cutting ability for fine sanding and smoothing or rubbing final finishes. It is widely available in grades fine through superfine.

Selecting the Right Sandpaper Wood finishing sandpapers are divided into two basic classes, cabinet papers and finishing papers. Each class is available in any of the abrasives described previously and has its specific purpose and appropriate use.

Cabinet sandpapers are generally used for sanding raw wood surfaces. They range in coarseness from very coarse to very fine. Finishing papers are used to create a uniform, smooth surface on a final finish or on raw wood, provided the surface has first been rough-sanded with a coarse cabinet paper. The finish paper removes the deeper scratches made by the coarse sandpaper.

When used properly, finishing papers will uniformly smooth each finish coat. The tiny, virtually invisible scratches produced will provide better adhesion of subsequent finish coats.

The backing to which the abrasive grit is glued can be paper, cloth, fiber, or a combination. Paper and cloth backings are the most widely used in wood finishing and refinishing. These backings are often available in waterproof versions. Waterproof papers are coated with only the finest grades of abrasives and are primarily used for rubbing the final finish to a satin smoothness.

Paper backing is moderately tough and is available in four thicknesses called weights: A, C, D, and E. The A-weight is a soft pliable grade of paper generally used for final sanding of raw wood or where flexibility is required. A-weight backings are used on finishing papers. C- and D-weight papers are medium weight papers and are used for rougher sanding jobs. This is the most common backing weight, used on most cabinet papers. E-weight is the heaviest, thickest paper that is only used occasionally in hand sanding for very rough sanding and shaping.

Cloth backing is available in two grades, J and X. J-grade is a lightweight cloth backing that is generally used for very fine sanding and rubbing the final finish. The heavier X-grade is primarily used with power sanders.

Paper backing is less expensive but has a tendency to crack; cloth backing is more flexible and may be more suitable to some sanding jobs. Each backing is available in several sizes and forms with a standard size of 9 × 11 inches being the most common. Sandpapers also come in strips, half-sheets, rolls, disks, drums, and belts. Abrasive sheets can be torn with the use of a steel rule or saw blade. Most sandpapers tear best across the short dimension.

The way in which the abrasive grit is glued to the backing is also a factor to consider when selecting sandpaper. There are basically two types of coatings, open-grain and closed-grain. Closed-grain papers have thickly applied abrasive grit that covers the entire surface; open-grain papers have abrasive grit that only covers about 60 percent of the surface, leaving space between the grains. Closed-grain papers sand faster but tend to clog easily. They are best used for sanding raw hardwood. Open-grain papers do not clog as easily, so they are more suitable to soft, gummy woods and finish removing.

Also consider the coarseness or fineness of the abrasive grit. Sandpaper grit is designated by grit number and grade. A single number indicates the grit number with 20 being the coarsest and 600 the finest. A fraction, ranging from 3½ to 10/0, denotes grade with 3½ being the coarsest and 10/0 being the finest. There are also word descriptions for various sets of grit numbers and grades. For example: a "1/0 - 80 D" paper means the grade is medium fine and has 80 grit with a moderately thick backing.

Another major consideration is the type of sanding being done. Initial shaping and rough sanding require the coarsest papers available. Rubbing and polishing the final finish requires the finest papers. The Abrasive Classification and Common Usage Chart indicates the best sandpaper for several common uses.

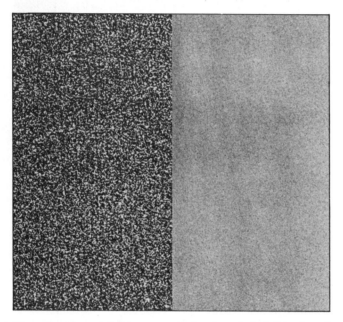

The abrasive at left is open grained and at right, closed grained.

Power or Hand Sanding

Sanding can be done by hand or by machine. Power sanding is much faster and far less tedious but requires special care. Hand sanding is slower but safer, generally resulting in a smoother final surface. If a power sander is left in one place for too long a time, the surface will be worn down unevenly; or if it is tilted to one side or the other, a ridge may be cut into the wood. With care and practice, however, the rapidly moving power sander can reduce time and effort substantially.

Hand Sanding Hand sanding has been the traditional method of smoothing wood for many years. As a wide variety of power sanding equipment became available, these machines were able to do as thorough a job as hand sanding for many jobs. Most professionals, however, prefer hand sanding for the final sanding of raw wood and finish coats.

Proper hand sanding requires some form of backing for the abrasive paper. Support from just the fingers or hand will not provide uniform sanding pressure which can result in an uneven surface. To achieve uniform pressure, a sanding block should be used for most jobs.

Sanding blocks can be made from wood scraps around the home or can be purchased in various sizes and styles from most paint and hardware stores. The best size sanding block is 3 × 5 inches and 1 to 1½ inches thick. It is best to use a block made of hardwood because it is strong, durable, and can be easily shaped to facilitate gripping. The sanding face of a hardwood block should be padded with a thin layer of felt, sponge, or rubber, particularly for finish sanding. This padding, glued to the block surface, helps disperse heat caused by friction which can cause the paper to clog. The padding also prevents loose grit from becoming trapped between the block and sandpaper. This can cause deep scratches across the finished surface.

For a 3 × 5 inch block cut a standard size sheet of

Abrasive Classification and Common Usage Chart

Use	Grit	Backings	Grade	Word Description
Initial finish removal	20 to 40	D	3½ to 1½	Coarse or very coarse
Rough sanding and shaping	60 to 80	D	½ to 1/0	Medium
Preparatory sandings— softwoods	100 to 120	A	2/0 to 4/0	Fine
Preparatory sandings— hardwoods	120 to 150	C	3/0 to 4/0	Fine
Finish sanding—softwoods	180 to 220	A	5/0 to 6/0	Very fine
Finish sanding—hardwoods	220 to 280	A	6/0 to 8/0	Very fine, extra fine
Dry-sanding sealers & finishes	220 to 280	A	6/0 to 8/0	Very fine, extra fine
Wet-sanding sealers & finishes	220 to 280	J or X	6/0 to 8/0	Very fine, extra fine
Polishing finish coat— all woods	280 to 400	J or X	8/0 to 10/0	Extra fine to superfine

abrasive paper into 4½ × 5½-inch quarters. Roll the paper from side to side, paper side down, over the edge of a bench or table to soften the paper and make it more pliable. Wrap one quarter of the abrasive paper around the bottom and sides of the block. Hold the block and loose edges of the paper securely with the thumb and fingers. Do not attempt to tack or nail the paper to the block.

As the paper becomes worn, shift it to present new edge surfaces or turn upside down to present an entire new sanding surface. Replace paper when wear becomes excessive.

The primary disadvantage of commercial sanding blocks is that most require special sizes of abrasive paper and do not utilize the entire grit surface. A blackboard eraser makes an excellent and relatively inexpensive sanding block.

Not all sanding is done on large flat surfaces, so all your sanding blocks should not be flat and rectangular. Many wood products have curves, ornate spindles or legs, molded edges, and so forth. To sand these confined areas, collect an assortment of sanding blocks of different sizes and shapes. You may have to design a special block to sand a particular area. Curved surfaces can be sanded with sandpaper-covered dowels, flexible materials, or angled blocks. Several types of abrasives, such as abrasive strips and abrasive cord, are also available for difficult areas.

Power Sanding There are several types of power sanders available. These sanders are excellent for efficient rough sanding and can be used for finish sanding; however, hand sanding generally produces a smoother final finish.

The four basic types of power sanders are finishing sanders, vibrating sanders, belt sanders, and disc sanders:

- Finishing sanders are the most useful in finishing and refinishing wood. They operate in one of three ways: orbital, straight line, or dual action. With orbital action the abrasive moves in a flat, light oval. The oval does cut across grain slightly, removing wood from the surface in a somewhat noticeable swirl pattern. This pattern must be sanded manually. Straight line sanders move back and forth in the direction the sander is moved, making it possible to sand entirely with the grain. Not much wood fiber is removed to assure a fine smooth finish. It offers a surface closest to that achieved with hand sanding in slightly less time. Dual action combines the motions of both orbital and straight line. Orbital can be used for rough sanding and the straight line for finish sanding. All finishing sanders work slowly.
- Vibrating sanders offer very smooth surfaces by providing fast, short orbital or straight line strokes. They are adequate for finish sanding but are very slow for heavy or rough sanding.

- Belt sanders are very fast straight line sanders. An abrasive belt revolves rapidly against the wood. This sander is difficult to use because of this fast cutting action. If it is left in one position for too long, an excessive amount of wood will be removed, causing a depression on the surface. But with practice, belt sanders can rough sand or strip wood in incomparable time.
- Disc sanders should not be used on fine wood products because they unevenly remove too much material very quickly. They leave large noticeable cross grain marks that are difficult to remove. When fitted with a buffing pad, the large commercial disc sander or the small one that attaches to a household power drill will buff a polish or wax to a high gloss.

When selecting a sander, consider several factors. The larger the pad area, the more work a sander can do. A smaller pad, however, may be more appropriate for small, tighter areas. Intended use should govern pad selection. Weight is another important factor because it affects pressure which, in turn, can affect speed and sanding efficiency. The weight of the sander alone plus the weight of your hand should be the only pressure required for smooth, efficient operation. Power sanding creates fine wood dust that can hamper breathing and vision, not to mention the mess it causes. Many sanders are available with dust-collector attachments that greatly reduce the amount of dust discharged into the atmosphere. Also consider the type of paper to be used. Generally, an open coat aluminum oxide or garnet paper works best for power sanding. Abrasive sheets of the exact dimension needed for most sanders are available at paint and hardware stores.

Proper Sanding Techniques

Sanding a wood surface is not difficult, but it is one of the most important preparatory steps so it must be done thoroughly and carefully. Before beginning, examine the surface to be sure that all imperfections or damages were repaired and that all of the previous finish, if any, has been removed. The basic sanding routine is as follows:

1. If a previous finish has been removed from the wood or if the surface is worn, begin sanding the raw wood with a fairly coarse abrasive paper (60-100 grit) to level ridges, wear marks, discolored areas, and filler from minor repairs. The coarseness of the paper depends on the type of wood; hardwoods require finer abrasives than softwoods. Use an open-coat paper on softwoods so clogging will not become bothersome. Too coarse a paper will damage wood fibers. Sand the entire surface uniformly at an angle with the grain. Never sand across the grain for normal surface preparation. Use straight strokes with

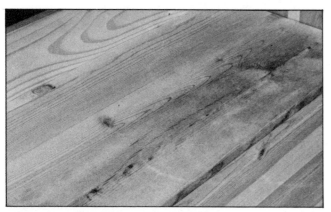

1. *An unfinished surface must be sanded.*

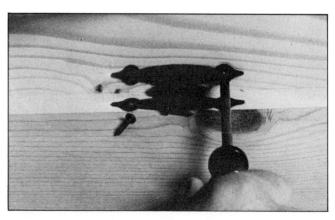

2. *Remove all hardware.*

3. *Begin sanding with a medium coarse abrasive (60-100).*

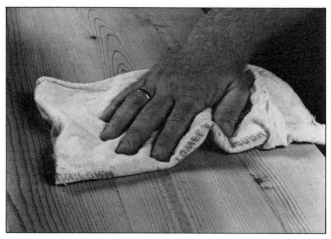

4. *Clean surface with dry cloth.*

moderate, even pressure. Between each sanding wipe all wood surfaces with a clean dry cloth or one slightly moistened with mineral spirits.

2. The initial sanding with coarse paper leaves many scratches on the wood surface. These scratches must be removed. Begin sanding with a medium grade paper (100-120 grit), again using even strokes with the grain. This sanding must be as uniform as possible if the finish is to have

5. *Sand with a medium to fine abrasive (120-220).*

even color and tone. If the wood is coarse and open-grained like oak or wormy chestnut, sanding directly with the grain may enlarge pores producing a rough surface that may even change the grain pattern. Sand at a slight angle to the grain to avoid enlarging the pores. Sand until all of the scratches created by the initial sanding have been removed. Avoid any cross grain scratches at this point.

3. Select a finer grade paper (120-220 grit) and sand with the grain. After this sanding the surface should be smooth enough to give a uniform reflection of light over the entire surface. Inspect surfaces closely by placing a light behind the surface to observe the reflection. Any irregularities should be clearly visible. Sand to remove them and examine surface again.

4. The final sanding is accomplished with a very fine abrasive paper (220-280 grit) or steel wool (2/0 or 3/0). Consider the type of finish you intend to use before selecting a fine abrasive. Painted or enameled surfaces need not be as smooth as varnished or shellacked surfaces. This step will give the wood its final degree of smoothness. It is essential that the sanding stroke has uniform length and pressure if a true flat surface is de-

6. *Use steel wool or very fine sandpaper for final sanding.*

7. *Clean surface with tack cloth.*

sired. After this sanding the surface is virtually ready to be stained and finished. During this step several techniques can be applied to achieve a special surface effect, including grain raising with moisture, applying a sanding sealer, or bleaching the wood. These techniques are explained later in the chapter.

Sanding Tips Now that you are familiar with the basic sanding procedure, the following tips are included to make the job easier and the results more professional looking:

- Do not cut sandpaper with sharp tools. The abrasive grit will dull their cutting edges. Fold and tear sandpaper with a straight edge or over a corner of a table.

- Abrasive paper should be changed frequently when worn; however, papers can be cleaned by tapping the block on a hard surface to shake loose dust, or clogged dust can be removed with a soft brush. This prolongs cutting ability.

- Even if a stripped wood surface appears or feels clean, sanding is required to remove wax or chemical residues.

- If you work on a wood product with many identical moldings, devise a felt-covered block that will enable you to uniformly sand these areas.

- To sand small corners and crevices, fold a small piece of abrasive paper and insert corner into a crevice and sand. As grit wears off fold, refold, and continue sanding.

- Regular sanding blocks do not work well on concave or convex curved surfaces. For concave surfaces, wrap the abrasive paper around a wooden dowel that is close to the size of the curved surface, and sand. Convex surfaces may be sanded with a block that has been hollowed out to accept the curved surface or by holding a piece of abrasive paper over a thick piece of flexible carpeting. Sand curved surfaces carefully to avoid damaging the fine contours.

- Turned surfaces, such as chair spindles or legs,

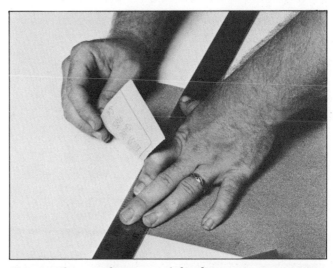

Tear sandpaper along a straightedge.

For sanding corners or crevices, fold a small piece of sandpaper and sand.

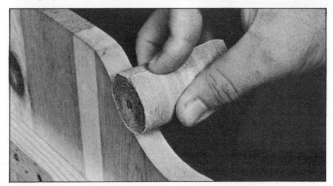

Devise an appropriate block for curved surfaces.

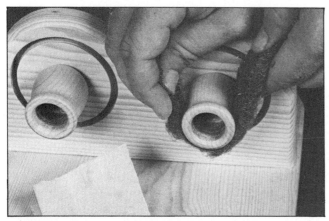

The shoeshine sanding technique.

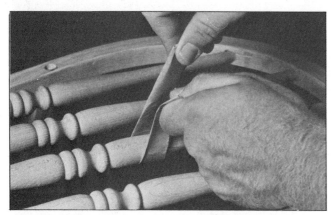

Using the shoeshine technique with sandpaper is good for round surfaces.

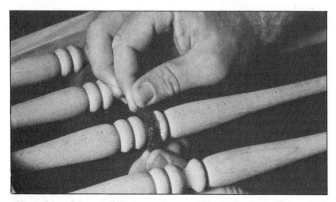

The shoeshine technique is excellent for small curved grooves or crevices.

Always sand with the grain, keeping the sanding block level with the surface.

Use steel wool when sanding against grain.

are best sanded with narrow strips of a fine grade abrasive paper worked back and forth across the surface in a shoeshine technique. Tape the back side of the paper to increase strength. Many times turned surfaces have grooves or channels cut into them. These can be sanded with abrasive cord. Steel wool may be more acceptable than sandpaper on most curved or turned surfaces. The shoeshine technique will work with steel wool as well.

- Use only the very fine abrasives for sanding the edges and ends of wood surfaces. The edges must be true and corners square. When sanding the top surface near the edge, do not allow the sanding block to extend more than one fourth its length beyond the edge or a rounded corner may result. Apply pressure on the back of the block to prevent the corners from becoming rounded. When sanding an end or edge surface, clamp two pieces of wood flush with the end to be sanded. The boards serve as guides to prevent the corners from being rounded and ensure a straight, uniform surface.

- Finish does not adhere well to sharp corners or edges. Sand sharp edges with a fine sandpaper to create and give the finish a better surface to adhere to. Use light, even strokes.

- When sanding across grain cannot be avoided, use steel wool rather than an abrasive paper. Steel wool is less likely to scratch the surface as deeply as sandpaper might.

- With the surface sanded to an acceptable smoothness wipe the entire surface with a tack rag to remove all dust and dirt. A tack rag picks up dust without leaving any residue on the wood surface.

To improve stain adherence, sand sharp edges.

Steel Wool

As an abrasive, steel wool has several advantages over sandpaper. Steel wool is made of fine intertwined steel strands that produce minute, sharply cut shavings without scratching the wood surface. It achieves a much smoother surface than sandpaper because it scrapes rather than cuts. Steel wool is also more flexible, is easier to clean, and can be used wet or dry.

Steel wool's major disadvantage is the tiny metal shavings that are produced as the pad disintegrates through use. These shavings are hard to detect but must be removed from the surface, generally with a damp cloth. If the metal shavings are not thoroughly removed, they can stain the wood, particularly oak. They are sharp and can also penetrate the skin or blow into the eyes. The use of rubber gloves and safety goggles is advisable.

Steel wool is widely available in several grades ranging from coarse to superfine. It is usually available as a long wide ribbon in economical roll form. The following chart identifies the grades commonly used in wood finishing and refinishing.

The above grades of steel wool are (from left to right): 3 coarse, 1 medium, 0 medium fine, and 000 extra fine.

Steel Wool Selection Chart

Name	Grade	Use
Superfine	0000	Very fine smoothing, polishing last coat of finish, rubbing topcoat
Extra fine	000	Smoothing finish surfaces, cleaning metals, spot removal
Fine	00	Rough smoothing for dull or high-gloss finish
Medium fine	0	Most common grade, smoothing, stripping
Medium	1	Coarsest grade used in wood finishing and refinishing
Medium coarse	2	Smoothing rough lumber
Coarse	3	Roughest grade, many industrial uses

Steel wool works best on hardwoods and areas which are nearly impossible to reach with stiff abrasive papers, such as turnings, ornate spindles, and carvings. It works rapidly and can be used with greater success than sandpaper on areas where sanding with the grain is not always possible. Steel wool is excellent for smoothing end grain surfaces after they have been sanded with an abrasive paper. After removing finish remover from wood with a putty knife or rag, you may clean off the messy residue with steel wool dipped in alcohol. The steel wool will not scratch the surface when wet.

Grain Raising

When wood comes in contact with moisture, the wood fibers become wet, swell, and rise above the surrounding surface; then they dry and become stiff. Once dry, these fibers never return to their original positions; therefore, it is important to reduce the effects of this grain raising before the final sanding and applying of the finish. This increases the wood's ability to withstand changes in dampness. Should the grain rise after the finish has been applied, the surface would have a rough, uneven texture; and the overall appearance would be ruined.

To avoid this, the wood fibers should be deliberately raised before final sanding is completed. This step is essential if you plan to use a water stain. This is accomplished by a process called sizing. Wood can be sized in a number of ways.

The easiest method is to thoroughly dampen the wood with clean water and a sponge or cloth. The water causes wood fibers to swell and raises the tiny loose end fibers called whiskers. Some woods whisker more than others. Allow the dampened surface to dry completely—overnight if you can spare the time. As the wood dries the fibers stiffen and rise above the surrounding surface. They can then be lightly sanded with the same grade of abrasive paper you would use for the final sanding. Be careful not to use too much water on veneers. Excessive moisture can loosen water-soluble veneer glues.

Actual size is made by dissolving glue in water until

1. Brush or wipe water onto surface.

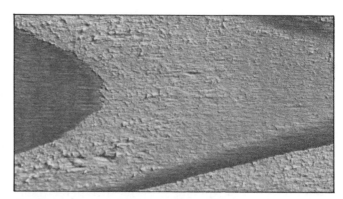

2. When dry, wood fibers will be raised.

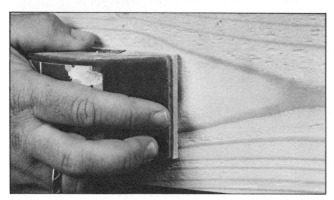

3. Sand raised fibers thoroughly, using progressively smoother grades.

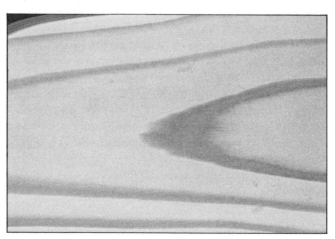

4. The smoothed surface is ready for sealing, staining, bleaching, or finishing.

it reaches a thin, runny consistency. One ounce of liquid glue to one pint of water is an adequate mix. This solution is then applied to the wood surface with a rag or sponge. The size causes the wood fibers to rise and stiffen. The wood fibers can then be sanded smooth. This process reduces the chance of grain raising in later stages and serves as a sealer coat for softer areas. It allows the stain to be applied more uniformly. Sizing is considered part of wood preparation and is not intended to be a filler or sealer.

Another method of raising and stiffening wood fibers is by applying a sanding sealer.

Sanding Sealer A sanding sealer functions in the same way as sizing. As wood is sanded with progressively finer grades of abrasive paper, the wood becomes increasingly smoother until it reaches a point where additional sanding will raise more wood fibers. If additional smoothing is required, a sanding sealer must be used. When you brush on a sanding sealer and allow it to dry thoroughly, the raised fibers stiffen and the entire surface hardens making the wood capable of being sanded to a greater degree of smoothness. The sanding agent in the sealer allows clean, powdery sanding without gumming the abrasive paper.

Sanding sealers are available in ready-mixed form or can be made by diluting shellac with three to four parts denatured alcohol. Ready-mixed sanding sealer should be stirred well and applied evenly over the surface. Allow to dry two to three hours and sand lightly with a very fine abrasive. Shellac solution should be brushed on smoothly, allowed to dry at least one hour, and then sanded.

Do not use sanding sealers indiscriminately. They do seal the wood somewhat which affects the wood's ability to accept stain and other finishing materials. If you must control the penetration of finishing materials run tests on similar wood to determine the effect of the sealer on the materials you plan to use.

Sanding sealer is another way to raise grain.

Bleaching

Bleaching is a process used to lighten the color of wood by using chemicals to remove some or all of the natural pigmentation. Bleaching does not affect grain pattern and tone, only color intensity. This process has several useful purposes. If an old finish penetrates deeply into wood pores, the wood will be darker than its original natural color even after stripping. The coloring of unfinished wood or stripped wood may be uneven or darker than desired. Through use and aging, wood can become darkened or it can be stained by weather, rust, water, or several other agents. Bleaching will lighten the wood in each of these cases to provide a uniformly colored surface. Sometimes discolored or stained areas may barely be visible on a raw wood surface, but as successive finish coats are applied and allowed to dry, the area will become more prominent.

Apply bleach before the final sanding. Bleach can raise the grain because of its liquid nature and generally leaves a residue. Raised wood fibers and residue must be sanded off. This can be accomplished with the final sanding. Bleaching requires a clean raw wood surface, free from dirt, oil, grease, and old finishing materials that can prevent the bleach from effectively lightening the wood. The wood surface is usually clean after rough, preparatory sanding. The bleaching effect will penetrate deep enough into the surface to permit final sanding. When bleached, the wood can be sanded and finished as you would any other wood.

Some woods bleach more easily than others. Generally, the darker, denser, or greasy woods are difficult to bleach. Multiple applications or a more concentrated solution may be required. The following chart indicates the bleaching qualities of certain woods. Many of the woods in the "Easily Bleached" category are so light that bleaching should be done only to remove stains.

Types of Bleach

There are several types of bleach that are suitable to wood finishing and refinishing for lightening wood and removing stains. The chemicals in all bleaching solutions are strong and can be extremely harmful. Skin or eye contact can cause injury, and the fumes are dangerous to breathe. Work in a well-ventilated area, wear rubber gloves, and protect your eyes, skin, and clothing from coming in contact with the bleaching solution.

There are two basic types of bleaching solution, home prepared solutions and commercially prepared solutions. Simple home prepared solutions are very effective on lighter woods and for spot-bleaching stains. They will lighten dark wood somewhat, but generally the stronger commercial bleaches available at most paint and hardware stores do a more thorough job. Commercial bleach, however, is hard to control when spot-bleaching. In the following section, the common home prepared bleaches are described first, and then commercially prepared bleaches are discussed.

Oxalic Acid This bleach is inexpensive, easy to make, and readily available in crystal form at most drug, paint, and hardware stores. Oxalic acid is an excellent mild bleach that is best suited to removing stains, particularly those left by the stripping process and lightening the color of lighter woods. The effect depends on the strength of the solution.

Standard oxalic acid bleach is created by dissolving 3 or 4 ounces of oxalic acid crystals in 1 quart of hot water. This creates a mild bleach that effectively removes stripping stains. For less bleaching use oxalic acid crystals in weaker solution. If extra bleaching is required, the standard solution can be followed with a solution of sodium hydrosulfite (photographer's hypo) and water. Add 2 to 4 ounces of hypo to 1 quart of hot water, depending on the darkness of the wood and the amount of lightening desired. A third solution, 1 ounce of borax in 1 quart of hot water is an alkaline wash that will destroy remaining traces of acid left on the bleached raw wood surface.

The bleaching sequence is as follows:

1. Apply the warm standard oxalic acid bleach solution carefully and evenly over the wood surface with a sponge or a brush with synthetic fibers. Bleach will destroy natural fiber brushes. Always apply bleach in the direction of the wood grain.

2. When the surface is adequately covered, allow to dry approximately 5 minutes. If the wood is sufficiently lightened, allow to dry thoroughly and

Bleaching Qualities of Common Woods				
Easily Bleached		**May Require Multiple Applications**	**Very Difficult to Bleach**	
Ash	Hickory	Mahogany	Cedar	Redwood
Beech	Maple	Oak	Cherry	Rosewood
Birch	Pine	Teak	Chestnut	
Elm	Spruce	Walnut	Ebony	

These common materials can be used to significantly lighten a dark or stained wood surface.

1. Apply oxalic acid bleaching solution evenly over the wood surface.

rinse with clean water. Allow wood to dry overnight before sanding. If the color has not lightened satisfactorily after the 5 minutes, apply another coat of the standard solution, allow to dry, and rinse. Repeat as necessary. When the wood reaches the desired color, the final rinse should be the borax solution followed by water.

3. If any unevenness of color should occur, apply the standard solution to the darker areas. Over-bleaching should not be a concern. The wood can be darkened by staining. Do not flood the surface with bleach; this can cause uneven lightening.

4. If after several applications of the standard solution the wood has not been lightened enough, you will have to apply another coat of standard oxalic acid solution, allow to dry about 5 minutes, and then apply a coat of the hypo solution. The hypo solution intensifies the bleaching action. Allow the second application to dry about 10 minutes, wash with borax solution to neutralize the bleach, rinse with clean water, and allow to dry overnight before final sanding and finishing.

Hydrogen Peroxide This is a common bleach that is very effective in bleaching wood. The hydrogen peroxide used in this bleach is not the 3 percent solution commonly used in the home as an antiseptic but is a concentrated 30 percent solution available from wood-finishing supply houses and drug stores. It is considerably more expensive than other home prepared bleaches, but it will lighten most of the darker woods effectively.

1. Dissolve 3 or 4 ounces of lye in 1 quart of hot water and apply solution over entire surface of

wood with a sponge, cloth, or synthetic bristled brush. Allow to dry 20 to 30 minutes.

2. Apply hydrogen peroxide full strength to the surface and allow to dry. As the surface dries, the color should become lighter.

3. Rinse thoroughly and allow to dry overnight. Hydrogen peroxide does not need to be neutralized.

Household Laundry Bleach Chlorinated liquid laundry bleach (Clorox) is very mild but effective for removing stains from wood or for lightening woods, such as pine, gum, maple, and walnut. Household ammonia is equally as effective as laundry bleach. These products are not suitable for dark woods.

1. Apply the bleach or ammonia full strength to the spot or wood surface.

2. Allow the material to dry for 15 minutes and wash with clean water. If the desired color has not been attained, repeat the application. Each application will lighten the color further.

3. When all applications have been made and the desired color is reached, wash the wood thoroughly and allow to dry overnight or longer.

Commercial Wood Bleaches The best and most efficient bleaches are commercially prepared solutions that are available at most paint and hardware stores. They are generally two-solution preparations which can be applied in succession or mixed together and then applied. The first solution is a caustic alkali and the second, a strong hydrogen peroxide. Some one-solution preparations are available. Most commercial bleaches contain strong, caustic chemicals and are best suited for overall surface work. Spot-bleaching is

2. If the standard solution does not lighten the wood, apply hypo after bleach.

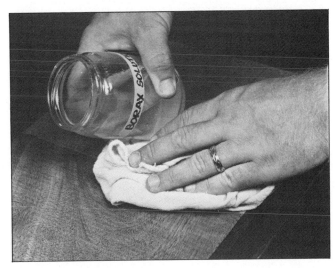

3. When wood is lightened apply borax solution to neutralize bleach.

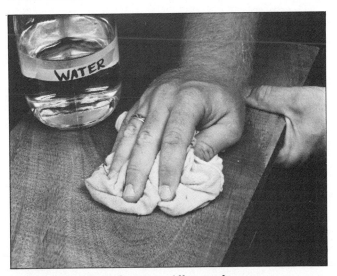

5. Rub with clean dry rags. Allow to dry.

4. Rinse the entire surface carefully with clean water. Do not flood glued areas.

very hard to control. Some of these bleaches may remove all or most color in a single application. In any case, carefully follow the manufacturer's directions on the label and take the necessary precautions to protect skin, eyes, lungs, and clothing.

1. Apply the first bleaching solution evenly to the wood surface in the direction of the grain with a brush, rag, or sponge. Allow to dry 15 minutes or longer depending on the manufacturer's directions.

2. Apply the second bleaching solution in the same

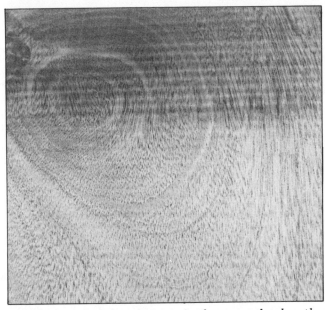

The top section of mahogany is the natural color; the bottom section is the bleached color.

manner over the first solution but with a different brush, rag, or sponge. It is the reaction between the two solutions that causes the wood to bleach.

3. Allow the surface to dry, preferably overnight, and wash with clear water or a neutralizing solution if recommended in the directions. Allow to dry overnight before final sanding.

4. If the wood has not been sufficiently lightened, repeat the entire process.

NOTE: Each manufacturer's directions may vary. Read labels carefully and follow the directions closely.

To assure proper bleaching of wood surfaces consider the following recommendations:

- Mix all solutions in glass containers; metal can cause discoloration of wood surfaces. Store in cool, shaded area.

- Be sure to rinse or neutralize all chemical residues before continuing the finishing process.

- Exposing a wet bleached surface to sunlight will intensify the bleaching process.

- Protect the floor and surrounding area of your work space from bleach spills or splatters.

- If the surface begins to lighten too much shortly after application of the bleach, flooding the surface with vinegar will stop the bleaching action immediately.

- A properly bleached surface will accept any finish, but penetrating oil and polyurethane are the most popular.

- All bleaches raise the grain of the wood slightly. Sand bleached surfaces with very fine sandpaper to achieve proper finishing smoothness. Do not sand more deeply than the bleach has penetrated.

Final Examination If you have carefully followed the steps outlined in this chapter, your wood product—whether unfinished or previously finished—is ready to be stained or naturally finished. But first examine the entire wood surface closely. Have all the surface imperfections and damages been repaired? Has the surface been thoroughly sanded to remove dirt and residues? Is the surface smooth? Is the wood color the proper tone? Have all stains been removed? If you can answer these questions with a definite yes, you are ready to move to the next finishing steps.

Staining Wood

Now that you have spent considerable time and effort to properly prepare the wood surface, you are probably quite anxious to showcase your hard work by applying a new finish. Before you begin brushing on that first coat of clear finish, look closely again at the raw wood surface. Is this the actual color you want to show through a clear final finish?

Let's assume that after stripping the old paint off the project in front of you, you discover a fine piece of maple furniture. You have long admired the beautiful maple finishes on other pieces in furniture stores or in friends' homes, but the color of your bare wood surface does not appear as warm and the grain pattern does not seem as pronounced. Will the finish alone achieve the traditional maple look? Probably not.

Most finishes do not appreciably change the color of wood. A clear finish only slightly darkens the natural wood color. A simple test to determine the approximate color a wood will have when a clear finish is applied is to wet a small area of the surface slightly with clean water. The resulting color should resemble the finished color. Dry, porous softwoods will change the most. Unseasoned woods will show little change. Woods with open pores darken under a clear finish to a greater degree than woods with closed pores.

Raw wood has two natural colors. Wood fresh from the sawmill or lumberyard has a clean, pale look. But as that wood dries and ages, it darkens and develops a richer character in response to oxidation and exposure to light. This attractive quality (called patina, as previously mentioned) is highly desirable, and most furniture manufacturers, in an effort to make their products more appealing to the consumer, try to achieve this appearance by using a stain. This is why the maple finishes you have admired look so different from your bare wood surface.

Almost all finished wood is color controlled to some degree through the use of stains. If, however, your project has well-developed patina that you were able to carefully preserve during each step of surface preparation, the color should not be altered. A rich, one hundred-year-old patina cannot be reproduced, but through staining the richness of color and definition of grain of such a patina can be successfuly imitated.

Why Stain Wood?

The traditional finished color that is associated with a particular species of wood is generally not the natural color of the raw wood. The colors we accept and desire as the standard colors for specific woods are usually achieved by applying a stain and clear finish coat over the natural color and texture of the surface. The stain penetrates the wood surface changing the color of the wood near the surface but, at the same time, allowing the grain to be seen quite clearly. Staining has a transparent effect that only changes color, never the grain pattern.

Rich dark woods, such as walnut, mahogany, teak, and cherry have naturally beautiful color that does not require staining. Staining can enhance the natural hues, but it is not essential. Woods that have developed patina through aging also seldom require staining. Pine, maple, oak and birch all develop a golden color through aging. However, most medium and light-colored woods need a stain to create beautiful color and striking character. Even if the raw wood surface color is appealing to you, a light stain can strengthen color and highlight grain, improving the overall appearance.

You can do several things with stain:

- You can stain wood to create its accepted traditional color which is generally darker and richer than the natural hue.
- You can stain to make one wood look like another. Common, inexpensive woods that have little color or character can be stained to resemble the general appearance of popular fine hardwoods. For example, gumwood is a common, relatively inexpensive furniture wood, and although uninteresting in the natural state, it can be stained to look like walnut, cherry, or even mahogany. It is hard to detect a quality imitation stain job without closely examining the grain pattern. This is particularly useful if you are trying to refinish a piece to match other pieces of furniture constructed of a different wood. Many pieces of furniture are constructed of several kinds of wood. Staining can blend the natural colors of the different woods into one uniform color.
- You can stain wood to give it an older appearance. Whether you have a new piece of unfinished furniture or a piece that has lost its natural patina through stripping, proper staining can give an artificial patina that looks many years older than it actually is.
- You can add character to any wood by staining. Woods which naturally lack color and character or have faded or have been bleached will be greatly enhanced by staining. Staining emphasizes grain patterns and creates a warm, almost glowing, appearance.

Staining of Common Woods		
Woods That Have Little Color and Should Be Stained	**Light Woods That Can Be Stained or Finished Naturally**	**Woods with Good Color That Do Not Require Stain**
Basswood, Fir, Gumwood, Poplar, Pine, Spruce	Ash, Aspen, Maple, Beech, Oak, Birch, Cedar, Mahogany, Wormy Chestnut, Elm, Hemlock, Sycamore, Redwood	Butternut, Rosewood, Maple, Cherry, Teak, Hickory, Mahogany, Ebony, Walnut

Staining is not an essential refinishing step but only a way of controlling the wood's color by strengthening or altering it. It does not provide a protective coating for the wood surface. To protect the wood from moisture, dirt, and shock, and to prevent the stain from fading, a clear protective finish coat must be applied. Several finishing materials have color added to them, but these colors are not as transparent as the colors in stains.

Choosing the Right Color

There are many types of stains on the market in hundreds of colors. By knowing the advantages and disadvantages of each type, you can select a stain to solve any conceivable problem or achieve any desired result. But first you must know what you want the final color to be and how it will make the wood look.

Almost all quality hardwoods and some softwoods have a color that is considered the traditional color for that species of wood, and some woods look better when stained a particular color. But the only right color is the one that best meets your needs and desires.

The best way to become a good judge of wood color is to examine wood finishes in furniture stores, at antique shows, or in magazines. Determine which colors you find especially appealing and which will best enhance the style of the piece you plan to refinish.

In the past, craftsmen mixed their own stains with pigments before stain manufacturers began to offer a wide range of ready-mixed colors available in most paint and hardware stores. Color charts and even stained wood samples showing the various colors each manufacturer has can usually be found at these retail outlets. Each manufacturer has its own version or shade of a color, and these shades, even though they have the same name, vary greatly.

In addition to several unique shades or colors, most manufacturers produce several standard stains which are called by the names of the wood they represent. Each color then is subdivided into common shades. These standard colors and shades often include:

- Oak—light oak (golden yellow); dark oak (yellowish brown); golden oak (reddish brown).
- Maple—standard maple (yellowish brown); honey or amber (light reddish brown); Vermont (dark reddish brown).
- Mahogany—mahogany (reddish brown); dark mahogany (dark brownish red).
- Walnut—(very dark, from brown to almost black).

When selecting a stain, do not take these names literally. The name implies only a color. There is no standardization of names to describe colors from different manufacturers. A walnut stain applied to pine wood will not produce a very good imitation of an expensive, finely textured walnut wood. Any stain will produce totally different colors on two different woods. Regardless of the name on the can, a stain can be used on any wood to obtain a certain shade. It just depends on what you want the final product to look like.

Before purchasing a stain, test the color by dabbing a small quantity on a white piece of paper if the store will permit you to do this. If not, wipe some of the stain on a concealed area of your wood surface to see how the color develops and dries. The wet color differs from the dry color, and both colors may differ from the color chart or stained wood sample you saw at the store. If the color is acceptable, begin staining. If not, select another color and test, repeating the process until you find the right color.

Color can even vary from one can to another. If your project is large, buy enough cans of the stain to cover the entire surface, then mix all the cans together to insure a uniform color. If you cannot find an appropriate ready-mixed color, you can mix one or several colors of the same type of stain together to achieve the desired shade.

Selecting Wood Stain

There are several types of wood stains from which to choose, but selecting the proper one for your project can be a confusing decision. Each stain is intended for a specific use based on its own set of qualities. Before trying to select a stain, you should know what types of stains are available, the advantages and disadvantages of each, and how each one is applied.

Stain selection should be based on the following factors: how well the stain penetrates, ease of application, how clean and transparent the stain will be when it dries, and a reasonable drying time. The variety of wood and condition of the prepared surface can affect each of these factors. You must match the qualities you most desire with your project and the type of wood of which it's constructed. This will determine the type of stain you should buy.

In recent years, stain manufacturers have designed their products for use by the do-it-yourselfer. These stains are generally ready-mixed, easy to apply, and dry very quickly. This change by the industry has made some of the traditional staining methods obsolete to the occasional refinisher. Most of these time-honored methods, generally used by only the most experienced and dedicated craftsmen, involve hours of mixing and matching, are difficult to apply, and require a long drying time. In most cases they are no more durable or beautiful than the new stains.

With the exception of some very special uses, almost all staining needs can be taken care of by three basic types of stains: pigmented wiping stains, water stains,

and non-grain-raising stains. These three types of stains will be discussed individually. The other types will be discussed in a general section. Application techniques will be presented later in the chapter.

Pigmented Wiping Stain

This is a large, widely popular family of inexpensive stains that are available in many colors, forms, and packages: liquids, pastes, or creams which are packaged in cans, bottles, tubes, or spray cans. Minwax and Deft are popular brands. These stains have ground pigments suspended in a penetrating resin, water emulsion, or the latex-based vehicle. The penetrating resin helps seal the wood to a greater degree than the other vehicles. Because the pigments are suspended and not in solution, the stain must be stirred constantly to ensure an even distribution of pigment for a uniform color of the stained surface. The pigment is generally heavier than the vehicle and has a tendency to settle to the bottom of the container.

Pigmented wiping stains (not to be confused with pigmented oil stains) deposit pigments in wood pores, soft areas, and surface imperfections such as scratches, dents, and cracks. These stains greatly accentuate the grain pattern of the wood. Unless a distressed effect is desired, the surface must be carefully

Popular Stain Reference Chart

Feature	Wiping Stain	Water Stain	NGR Stain	Penetrating Oil Stain	Pigment Oil Stain	Alcohol Stain	Varnish Stain
Coloring Matter	Solid pigment	Aniline dye powder	Aniline dye powder	Aniline dye powder	Solid pigment	Aniline dye powder	Aniline dye powder
Solvent	Penetrating resin, water	Water	Alcohol	Mineral spirits or turpentine	Mineral spirits or turpentine	Alcohol	Varnish
Application Method	Brush	Brush or spray	Spray	Brush and wipe	Brush and wipe	Spray	Brush or wipe
Ease of Application	Easy	Very easy	Very easy	Difficult	Very easy	Easy	Easy
Drying Time	6-12 hours	8-12 hours	½-2 hours	24-30 hours	3-12 hours	¼-1 hour	8-12 hours
Cost	Inexpensive	Inexpensive	Expensive	Moderate	Moderate	Expensive	Moderate
Qualities:							
Transparent	Poor	Excellent	Good	Fair	Excellent	Fair	Poor
Bleeding	None	None	Very little	Very much	None	Very much	None
Grain Raising	Very little	Very much	Very little	None	None	Very little	None
Coverage	Uniform	Moderate	Moderate	Uniform	Uniform	Moderate	Uniform
Fading	Very little	None	None	Very little	None	Very much	Very little
Penetration	Deep	Very deep	Very deep	Deep	Not deep	Deep	None

and thoroughly smoothed, or blemishes will become very apparent.

Pigmented wiping stains work best on soft coniferous woods such as white, pine, spruce, and fir. These are the woods commonly used in the construction of unfinished furniture. These stains considerably darken soft porous woods such as pecan and fir because they are able to accept stain readily. Hardwoods, such as maple, birch, and cherry, do not absorb much stain, but open-pore hardwoods absorb a great deal of stain in the pores, creating a stunning, well-defined grain pattern. Wiping stains are not as suitable to fine-grained woods as either water stains or non-grain-raising stains.

Pigmented wiping stains have a feature that most other stains do not. Because the stain accumulates and penetrates deeply into wood pores, a blond or white wiping stain will actually lighten the surface of coarse-grained woods. The only other way to achieve a lighter wood color is through bleaching.

Size or a sanding sealer is commonly used on the wood surface before staining to reduce penetration, ensure uniform color, and to provide a smoother surface for the wipe-on property of the stain.

Water Stain

Water stains are very inexpensive, easy to use, and come in a wide variety of clear, brilliant colors. These stains are primarily used in professional or factory wood finishing and refinishing. Water stains are available at some paint and hardware stores but are usually ordered through the mail from one of several mail order wood-finishing supply houses.

Water stains are easily created by dissolving aniline dye powders in hot water according to the specifications on the dye package. The resulting concentrated solution can be stored indefinitely in glass bottles, can be diluted with water to create lighter shades, and can be intermixed with other water stain powders to create almost any color or shade imaginable. Water stains offer more pure colors and better color control than any other stain. The colors do not fade or bleed and can be applied to a wood surface without a sealer coat.

One of the most important features of a water stain is its permanent, deep, uniform penetration even in woods with varying porosity and density. However, water stains should only be used on new woods because any residue or remaining stain on a stripped surface often causes uneven penetration. These stains can be used on any new wood but work especially well on fine hardwoods where they penetrate slowly and thoroughly. Hardwoods which have a beautiful natural color that only needs slight enhancement, such as oak, cherry, or walnut, are particularly well suited to water stain.

Multiple applications can be brushed on to achieve darker tones without leaving overlap marks. Each coat slightly darkens the wood. This gradual buildup of color gives you excellent control over the final color. The color has an overall evenness; wood grain is neither accentuated nor subdued.

Although the advantages of water stains are considerable, proper use can be difficult for the novice. The primary disadvantage of water stains is that they cause the wood fibers to swell which raises the grain. This can cause a rough stained surface and adversely affect the final finishing process. To avoid this, the grain must be deliberately raised prior to staining as described in the previous chapter. You can lightly sand the raised fibers after staining, but you risk removing too much wood and color, causing uneven surface color.

Another disadvantage for the novice is mixing the solution. Although relatively easy to mix, more time and care is required to obtain the proper color than by simply opening a can of ready-mixed stain. And if you run short of water stain, it will be very difficult, if not impossible, to match the initial color.

Some aniline powders will dissolve in alcohol or a water-alcohol mix. This quality will be indicated on the label. Aniline dyes do not produce the same color when mixed with alcohol as they would when mixed with water. By altering the proportions of water and alcohol in the solution, a wider variety of colors is possible. These colors tend to be a bit cooler and more subtle. Alcohol will not raise the grain like water, but alcohol stains are harder to apply evenly because they dry quickly.

Non-Grain-Raising Stain

Although water stains are desirable because of their many advantages, they do raise the grain which requires a great deal of preparatory work before the stain can be applied. Finishing manufacturers have developed non-grain-raising (NGR) stains in an effort to retain many of the water-soluble stain's qualities while eliminating the grain-raising effect.

In NGR stains, the powdered aniline dyes are dissolved in an alcohol or a petroleum by-product solvent that will not cause the wood fibers to swell. Because they use solvents rather than water, NGR stains are more expensive, but they do save considerable surface preparation time.

NGR stains are available in powdered or ready-mixed form, but because they are considered industrial products, they are very hard to find at retail outlets. There are several reputable mail order finishing-supply houses that carry NGR stains. If you order powdered NGR stains, mix the solution carefully according to the instructions on the package. Ready-mixed NGR stains generally come in quart bottles. Except under special circumstances, these ready-mixed solutions are seldom used full strength. They can be thinned to the desired shade with wood alcohol or a solvent recommended by the manufacturer. There is a wide variety of ready-mixed colors available. To create a custom color, you can mix either ready-mixed tints or aniline powders.

Spraying is the recommended method of application as it will leave a thin, smooth, uniform coat of stain on the wood surface. The stain will dry in just a couple of hours. Additional coats can be added until the desired color is reached. You can slow down the quick-drying action of a NGR stain by adding a small quantity of water to the solution. Water does increase the chance of grain-raising but usually not to a significant degree.

Because NGR stains are very rapid-drying stains, achieving an even color by brushing is very difficult. Brushing also leaves more stain on the surface which can raise the grain slightly even though the stain is called non-grain-raising. Since NGR stains penetrate quickly and deeply, you may create a color that is too dark by applying the initial coat of stain too thickly.

NGR stains are the most widely used stains in the furniture and cabinetry industry. They work very well on most fine hardwoods and will darken these woods deeper and quicker than water stains. NGR stains should not be used on pine, spruce, fir or other soft-woods that have varying densities between spring and summer woods. These woods will absorb too much stain in some areas and not enough in others. The resulting grain pattern would be highly uneven and possibly too dramatic to be attractive.

Because NGR stains can darken quickly and un-evenly, test the stain you plan to use before applying it to the wood. If you apply the stain to a scrap of similar wood or an inconspicuous area of the project you are staining, you will be able to accurately judge how fast the stain dries and how even and dark the wood color will be after a single application.

Other Common Stains

Penetrating Oil Stains   There are two types of oil stains that are often confused with one another on dealer shelves; pigmented oil stains and penetrating oil stains. The major difference between the two oil stains is that pigmented oil stains are actually closer to thin paints because wood color is achieved by solid opaque pigments that settle into wood pores. Penetrating oil stains achieve color with a transparent solution that actually penetrates wood fibers to stain them.

Penetrating oil stains have largely been replaced by wiping stains. They are available at some paint and hardware stores in ready-to-use form in a fair variety of shades and are particularly well suited to the finisher without much experience. These shades are generally indicated on the container label or shown on a color chart. More than any other type of stain, a penetrating oil stain color will generally not vary from one can to another made by the same manufacturer. The stains are very easy to apply and will not raise the grain.

Penetrating oil stains are created by dissolving col-ored pigment powders or aniline dyes in a light oil, such as turpentine, mineral spirits, or benzol. Because the coloring matter in the solution is in liquid form rather than solid pigment form, the stains are trans-parent. The stain penetrates wood fibers deeply to quickly give the wood surface a clear transparent color that allows the natural beauty of the grain pattern to show through.

Penetrating oil stains can be used on any species of wood although they will not produce the same color on different woods. A golden oak stain will give the light golden brown color indicated on the color chart only to oak wood. When applied to a darker walnut wood, the final color will be considerably darker. Penetrating oil stains are used most effectively on woods with large open pores and coarse grain, such as ash, beech, cher-ry, chestnut, hickory, mahogany, oak, and walnut. The stain will not clog the pores, so the natural wood-grain pattern will not be concealed. These stains can be used effectively on smoother closed-grain woods, but the stain will not penetrate as deeply.

There are a couple of disadvantages common to penetrating oil stains. There are only a limited num-ber of shades available without mixing your own shade. Because the stains use oil-based solvents, they require a drying time of at least 24 hours before another coat can be applied. Penetrating oil stains penetrate deeply, particularly on soft porous woods. Removal of this stain is very difficult should re-finishing become necessary or desired.

Perhaps the greatest drawback of this stain is its tendency to bleed. When filler coats and some finish coats, especially varnishes or lacquers, are applied over penetrating oil stain, the oil softens and the color partially dissolves and mixes with the other coats, resulting in a muddy or spotted appearance. Bleeding can be avoided by applying a wash coat of shellac to seal the surface before the filler and finish coats are applied.

Pigmented Oil Stains   Commonly referred to as oil stains, pigmented oil stains are the easiest type of stain to apply and one of the most popular with home finishers. Apply the stain, wipe off the excess, and allow the project to dry.

Pigmented oil stains consist of finely ground solid pigments suspended in solution with mineral spirits, turpentine, or linseed oil. The pigments used in this type of oil stain are similar to those used in the manu-facture of paint. In fact, pigmented oil stains are actually closer to a thin paint than an actual stain.

Because the pigments are suspended in the solvent,

they tend to settle to the bottom of the container during storage and must be stirred frequently during application to ensure uniform color distribution. The pigments are also opaque, so they conceal or obscure the natural grain pattern of the wood. The pigments clog open wood pores which can give the surface a cloudy appearance.

Pigmented oil stains are nonfading, slow drying, and bleed less than penetrating oil stains. A wash coat of shellac should be applied before and after using a filler. Pigmented oil stains do not penetrate the surface; they simply cover the top layer of surface.

For best results use pigmented oil stains on pine, spruce, fir and other closed-grain softwoods. These softer, porous woods darken more than hardwoods because they absorb more of the stain. This type of oil stain can be used effectively on smooth, closed-grain hardwoods, such as beech, birch, cherry, gumwood, maple, and poplar. These woods will not absorb much stain because the wood pores are generally too small and close together to clog with the finely ground pigments. However, the pores of open-grained woods such as chestnut, mahogany, oak, and walnut will almost always clog.

Pigmented oil stains require very smooth surfaces to ensure even stain penetration. Any scratches, nicks, or dents will absorb more pigments, causing these irregularities to be accentuated. To improve uniformity of color on soft porous woods, apply a wash coat of linseed oil or shellac to the sanded surface prior to staining.

Spirit, or Alcohol, Stains Spirit stains are created by dissolving aniline dye powders in alcohol. They are available in ready-mixed liquid form or packages of aniline dyes and can usually be purchased through mail-order supply firms and mixed at home. Unlike the more common water stains, alcohol stains are available in limited colors; however, the selection is wide enough to meet most home-finishing needs. Spirit stains can be applied directly to a smoothly sanded surface. They will not swell wood fibers, so deliberate grain raising is not necessary.

The dyes will dissolve quickly in alcohol to yield a very clear stain. The concentration can be altered to change the intensity of a particular shade. Some dyes can be dissolved in either water or alcohol, some in just water, and others in just alcohol. Carefully read the label to make sure you have the correct dye for the solvent you plan to use.

Spirit stains dry very quickly by evaporation of the solvent, almost as soon as they are applied to the surface—particularly on raw wood. Because of the very rapid drying time, the stains are best applied by spraying. Brushing will work, but you must work quickly with long, even strokes. Avoid overlapping which will cause streaks. Large surfaces are best sprayed. Adding a little shellac to the stain will make brushing evenly slightly easier. The stain will be dry in less than one-half hour, leaving a brilliant transparent surface. These stains do not penetrate the wood deeply so they tend to fade with time, especially if exposed to direct sunlight. Finishing coats may reduce fading.

The major disadvantage of spirit stains are their extreme bleeding characteristics. They will bleed or dissolve into almost any finish coat unless the stain is properly sealed first. This bleeding will cause the finish to appear muddy. Alcohol will dissolve shellac, so a shellac wash coat should never be used beneath or over a spirit stain. Although bleeding is generally considered undesirable, this penetrating action can be useful in some instances. Spirit stains can be applied to an existing shellac, varnish, or lacquer finish. The stain will penetrate the surface and stain the surface beneath it. This can be useful in refinishing, touching up, or staining sap streaks.

Varnish Stains Varnish stains are quick, fairly inexpensive stains that should never be used on fine hardwoods. They are simply transparent aniline dyes dissolved in a varnish solvent that tend to obscure the natural wood color and grain pattern—particularly the darker stains. Varnish stains will not penetrate the wood surface, but they sit on the surface much like an enamel paint, leaving a cloudy, uneven finish.

Varnish stains are available at most paint and hardware stores in many ready-to-use popular wood shades. They dry in a few hours and generally do not fade when exposed to bright sunlight. Varnish stains are best used on cheaper grades of lumber with varying porosity because they give uniform coloring to such woods.

Wax Stains Several stain manufacturers have developed stains that penetrate, seal, and stain the wood with one application. The most familiar of these wax stains is probably Minwax. Wax stains consist of a penetrating oil stain mixed with wax and a drying agent. They come in a wide variety of colors that will dry to a rich, tough finish that enhances wood grain and color. They are applied easily with a cloth or brush and will not raise the grain. These stains will not fill wood pores, so an open grain effect is the result.

There are several other types of stains available, such as padding stains, toners, lacquer stains, latex stains, and glaze coats, but these are used for special effects or functions. Generally, all home finishing needs can be met with the eight stains described in this chapter.

Applying Wood Stains

The actual staining process is quite simple. Stain can be applied in a variety of ways: brushing, spraying, wiping, and sponging. The method you choose should be the one which will allow you to apply a specific stain in a manner that will achieve the most uniform coverage possible. Many factors can influence the way a particular stain is applied, but some general principles should be followed regardless of the stain being applied:

- Surface preparation is crucial. The surface must be smooth and free of all imperfections, residues, dirt, and oil. Stain will accentuate rough areas and scratches. If the surface is not clean, the stain will not cover evenly. See the previous chapter for proper surface preparation techniques.

- Some woods require sealing prior to staining. End grain, because it is more porous than other surfaces, should always be sealed to prevent overabsorption of stain. Woods with highly irregular grain patterns, uneven porosity, or large, open wood pores should be sealed. The sealed surface will permit smooth, uniform acceptance and penetration of the stain.

- Always work in a clean, dust-free area. Work under strong natural light, if possible.

- When you have selected the color you plan to use, test the color by applying it to an unexposed area of wood surface. You will acquire a feel for the stain: how dense it is, how easily it is applied, how well it penetrates, and how it dries. When you actually begin staining, start with the unexposed areas. By the time you reach the main exposed surfaces, you will have had plenty of practice to perfect your application technique.

- It is best to start with a lighter color; it is far easier to darken a surface than to lighten one. Less stain will result in a lighter color. In fact, two light coats are better than a heavy dark coat because heavy coats tend to brush on unevenly. Each successive coat of stain will also increasingly darken the wood. If the color is unacceptable, you can mix colors of the same stain type to create

End grain generally absorbs more stain than other surfaces. Sealing is required.

the desired tone. If you mix your own color be sure to make enough to completely cover the entire project. Remember, the finish topcoat will darken or intensify the stain color somewhat.

- Spraying is the method generally used by commercial finishers, and hand application is generally preferred by the home craftsman. In hand application, the stain is applied with a rag or brush. Excess stain is then wiped off with a clean cloth. These are essentially the only steps in staining wood, although techniques may vary from one type of stain to another. The depth and intensity of the color can be controlled by using different application techniques. For example, a cloth will not flood the surface with stain as much as a brush will.

- Apply all stains evenly to achieve uniform color on all surfaces. Avoid overlapping. Do not attempt to cover an entire piece at once. Work on small areas or on one surface at a time. Stain is best applied to horizontal surfaces, so try turning the piece to position working surfaces horizontally. If working on vertical surfaces is unavoidable, work from bottom to top and be sure to wipe off any runs, drips, or sags.

- Overlap only wet surfaces. If a dry surface is overlapped with wet stain, lap marks will be quite evident, particularly with water stains.

- There is no general rule as to when excess stain should be wiped off the surface; however, if you wait too long the stain will dry and be difficult to wipe off. If you don't wait long enough, you will probably remove too much color. The longer a stain remains on the surface, the deeper the stain penetrates and the darker the wood becomes. If you desire a lighter tone, the excess stain will have to be removed shortly after application. Most manufacturers recommend a drying time between coats on their product's label. Aside from this general recommendation, use your own judgment to determine when to wipe. When the color appears to be the proper tone, begin wiping. It is better to wipe off the excess too soon rather than too late. A second coat can always be added to darken the color, but the only effective way to lighten a surface is by bleaching. A small amount of color can be removed by hard wiping with clean rags or light sanding with fine steel wool. More color can be removed by wiping the surface with a solvent. When testing for color also keep track of drying time. Always wipe in the direction of the grain using a lint-free cloth. Carvings or decorative surfaces can be highlighted by wiping off excess stain sooner than the surrounding areas. Be careful not to remove too much stain from corners and edges.

- Allow stain to dry 24 hours unless otherwise specified. If a stain is not completely dry when a sealer coat or finish coat is applied, bleeding is likely to result. Do not sand a stained surface until after a sealer coat has been applied and allowed to thoroughly dry.
- Always follow manufacturer's instructions.

Stains come in many styles, colors, and types.

1. Brush on wiping stain liberally to ensure deep, uniform penetration.

Applying Pigmented Wiping Stains Pigmented wiping stains can be applied using any method, but brushing is usually the easiest. It is the wiping step that will determine the success of the job.

1. Pigmented wiping stains work best when applied over a wash coat. Mix equal parts of shellac and denatured alcohol. Brush over entire surface and allow to dry thoroughly. Sand lightly. Wipe away all dust.
2. Thoroughly mix the wiping stain. Brush the wiping stain on the prepared surface until it is completely covered. Allow the stain to penetrate.
3. When the stain begins to dull over, generally 5 to 10 minutes after application, begin wiping. The stain reaches its darkest tone when it begins to dull. If a lighter tone is desired, begin wiping sooner.
4. Wipe clean. Try to remove as much of the pigment from the wood surface as possible. Color is provided by pigment trapped in wood pores and the tiny invisible scratches created by sanding. If the color is too dark, lightly wipe the surface with a cloth dampened with paint thinner.
5. Allow to dry 12 hours or longer before applying finish coats. A single coat of varnish may be adequate to finish.

Applying Water Stains Aside from raising the grain, water stains offer more advantages to the home refinisher than any other stain. There is virtually no danger of overstaining with water stains because the stain can be diluted and the color built up gradually with multiple coats.

1. Deliberately raise the grain as described in the previous chapter.
2. Apply the water stain with a wide stiff nylon brush, brushing in the direction of the grain. Flood the surface with a full brush to ensure uniformity of application.
3. Generally, the stain is not wiped off. Excess stain will evaporate. If, however, the stain puddles, wiping lightly with a lint-free cloth is advised.

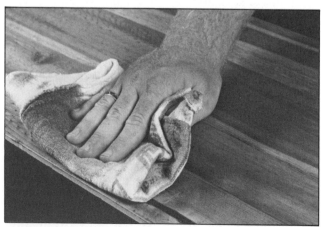

2. Wipe off excess with cloth.

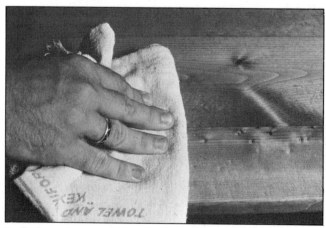

3. Rub surface with clean, dry cloth.

Water stains must be applied quickly and liberally. Water stains do not require wiping.

4. Allow the stained surface to dry for 12 to 24 hours.

5. If the grain has been raised slightly by the water stain, lightly sand the surface with very fine sandpaper in the direction of the grain. Remove dust.

Applying NGR Stains Non-grain-raising stains have many of the same advantages as a water stain, but, as the name implies, they do not raise the grain. This eliminates the time-consuming preparatory step of deliberately raising the grain. NGR stains dry in a matter of minutes, so the preferred method of application is spraying (see the special section on spraying in this chapter). Brushing is possible and effective if done with care. NGR stains are not as forgiving as water stains. Streaks and overlap marks are easy to make.

1. Wash the surface with NGR solvent.

2. Before the solvent dries apply the NGR stain with a relatively wide brush. Work quickly with a full wet brush. Work on small areas.

3. Avoid overlap marks. These streaks generally occur when wet stain is applied over the edge of a dry area.

4. It is best to apply multiple coats of weaker, thinned stain rather than one coat. This reduces brush and overlap marks.

5. The stain is ready for finishing in 2 to 4 hours.

Applying Penetrating Oil Stains Penetrating oil stains are easy to apply and control with wiping. Although it may be hard to locate a good penetrating oil stain initially, with practice a novice finisher can learn to completely control the effects of this stain.

1. Fill a wide, flat bristle brush with stain and apply with long even strokes in the direction of the wood grain. Continue until the working surface is completely covered with a moderately thin coat of stain.

2. Dampen a clean, lint-free cloth with the stain.

3. The darkness of the color depends on how long and how deep the stain is allowed to penetrate. If a light tone is desired, vigorously wipe off the excess stain shortly after application. Leave the stain in place longer if a darker tone is desired. Always wipe in the direction of the grain.

4. If some areas are lighter than the surrounding surface, reapply other coats of stain until the desired color is achieved. Wipe off excess.

5. Allow stain to dry at least 24 hours.

6. Sand very lightly to remove any roughness.

Applying Pigmented Oil Stains These are not true strains but more closely resemble thin paint. Proper surface preparation is essential to the success of pigmented oil stains.

1. Fill a stiff, flat bristle brush with stain. Apply to one section of the surface area. The stain can be brushed on in any manner or direction.

2. Wipe off excess stain with a soft, clean lint-free rag using uniform rubbing in the direction of the grain. The intensity of color is controlled by how vigorously you wipe off the excess stain.

3. If an area is too light reapply stain to the area and wipe carefully to blend the area into the surrounding surface.

4. If an area is too dark, some of the color can be removed by gently wiping the area with a cloth soaked in turpentine.

5. Allow the stain to dry 12 to 24 hours.

Applying Spirit Stains Spirit stains dry very fast, so spraying is the recommended application technique (see the special section on spraying in this chapter.) If, however, you do not have access to quality spraying equipment or would simply like to brush on the stain, brushing will prove satisfactory.

1. Fill a flat bristle brush to capacity.

2. Apply stain to surface using quick, long, even strokes in the direction of the grain. Work fast and avoid overlapping.

3. The more you work a spirit stain, the darker it becomes. If you have difficulty applying the stain, add a small amount of shellac to the stain to improve brushing.

4. Allow the stain to dry 1 hour. Seal surface before finishing.

Spray Finishing Stains

Spraying saves time, effort, and money, provided the proper technique is used. Spray finishing is much faster than brushing in the application of all finishing materials. In addition, many of the new quick-drying stains and finishes cannot be brushed effectively.

Basic spraying equipment consists of a spray gun attached to a suitable compressor by a hose. There are several types of guns and compressors that can be purchased or rented. Select the unit that will most efficiently do the job for you depending, of course, on type of finish and size of the project. A hardware salesperson or the manager of a rental shop should be able to supply you with the proper unit for your project.

Precautions

- Fumes are flammable and harmful to breathe. Work in a well-ventilated area and wear a respirator. Do not work near sources of flame.
- Spread newspapers or drop cloths to protect the area from overspray.
- Wear old clothing that will completely cover the skin.

Preparation

- Prepare and smooth the surface as you would for brush application.
- Thoroughly mix the stain or finish to evenly distribute the pigment or aniline dyes. Add the proper thinners as indicated by the manufacturer on the product container label.
- Strain the material to remove lumps and foreign matter that can clog the spray nozzle.
- Test the spray pattern on a piece of cardboard. The pattern should be round or oval shaped with a uniform distribution of the material. If the material spits out, it is too thick. If it runs, it is too thin. If the shape is not round or oval, adjust or clean the nozzle until the desired pattern is achieved.
- Practice by spraying a cardboard box or two. This will enable you to acquire a feel for the spray gun and the technique required for uniform coverage.

Spraying

- The spray gun will have to be tilted at a 45 to 60 degree angle to the surfaces being sprayed. Only fill the cup a little over halfway. If possible, tip the piece on its side to avoid tilting the gun.
- Hold the nozzle 6 to 10 inches from the surface to be sprayed. If the nozzle is too close, runs will result; if too far away, the surface will not be adequately covered.
- Using a proper stroke requires a flexible wrist. Move the nozzle in long strokes parallel with the work surface. This will distribute the paint evenly. If you try to make a long stroke with a stiff wrist, you will create an arc motion, and the paint will be distributed thickly in the center of the stroke and thinly at the ends of the stroke.
- Pull the trigger immediately prior to beginning a stroke and release it just after the end of the stroke. While spraying, keep the sprayer moving.
- Use straight, uniform horizontal strokes across the entire width of the surface. Move back and forth, making sure that each stroke overlaps half the previous stroke. This ensures good, uniform coverage without streaks, runs, or bare areas.
- To avoid overspraying which wastes finishing materials, spray the vertical edges of a flat surface first. This is called banding. You can then bring the horizontal strokes just to the edge of the surface without overspraying and achieve full uniform coverage.
- When spraying a piece of furniture plan the spraying sequence carefully to avoid overspray which can harm previously sprayed surfaces.
- Spray edges and corners first, overlapping both sides of the corner or edge.
- Mask any surfaces you do not want stained or finished. Remove masking material and/or tape as soon as possible.
- Cardboard can be used to catch overspray when spraying thin surfaces or to protect other areas from the spray.
- For spraying table legs, begin with the inner surfaces, then move to the outer surfaces. Adjust the spray to avoid excessive overspray and use a vertical stroke.

Cleanup

- Never allow finishing materials to dry in the spray gun.
- Pour remaining finish or stain from cup and fill about half full with the proper solvent (latex—water, shellac—alcohol, oil-based stain—paint thinner, lacquer—lacquer thinner).
- Spray until the cup of solvent is empty and all materials are cleaned from nozzle.
- Disassemble the spray gun and clean the individual parts with clean solvent.
- Allow to dry and then reassemble.

Proper Brushing Techniques

Brushing is the traditional method of applying stain and finishing materials to wood surfaces. Spraying is quicker, but the expense of purchasing a compressor and spray gun is quite high and unnecessary for occasional finishing jobs.

Quality brushes do make a difference in the way finishing materials are applied and the way they appear when dry. Good brushes will lay down a smooth, even coat, will hold more liquid, and will allow you to do the work with less effort and greater success.

Selecting a Brush

- The brush should have bristles of varying length. Bristle length should be 1½ times the width of the brush.
- Natural bristles will last longer than synthetic bristles, but natural bristles are considerably more expensive.

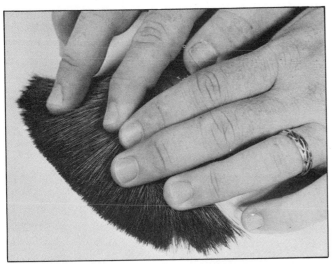

The bristles should be of varying lengths and frayed.

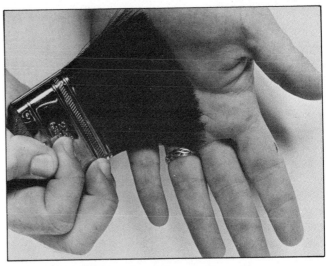

Bristles should spread evenly over the palm.

- Bristle tips should be frayed or split to enable the brush to hold more liquid.
- The bristles should feel soft and silky. They should spread evenly when pressed on the palm of your hand and spring back quickly when the pressure is stopped.
- The bristles should be securely fastened to the brush with a strong epoxy glue. If you loosen several bristles by fanning the brush, select a different brush.
- The bristles should form a chisel shape, created by arranging the longest bristles in the center of the brush with increasingly shorter bristles on either side.
- Brushes ranging in size from 1 to 3 inches are generally used for wood refinishing.

Application

- Hold the brush as you would a pencil. Grip the metal ferrule with the fingers and rest the brush handle between the thumb and index finger.
- Do not dip the brush into the finishing material

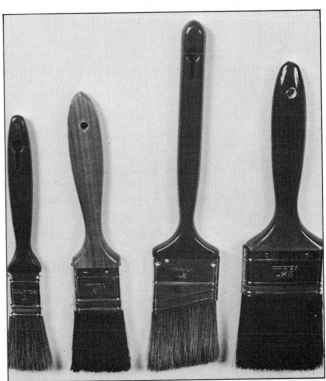

A variety of brushes can be used for finishing. An assortment of sizes and bristle types is best. From left to right: 1-inch natural bristle brush, 1½-inch synthetic bristle brush, 2-inch natural bristle brush with angled end, and a 2½-inch synthetic bristle brush for large flat surfaces.

more than ½ the length of the bristles.

- Do not remove excess material on the edge or lip of the container. Squeeze off excess on inside of can above liquid level.
- Use long steady strokes with moderate pressure. For large surface areas brush with and against the grain to assure uniform coverage. All final brush strokes should be in the direction of the grain. On the completion of a stroke, gently lift the brush from the surface.

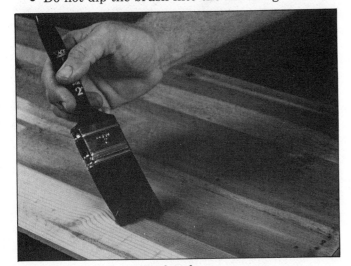

The proper way to hold a brush.

Always brush around turnings.

- Always brush around turnings.
- Use only the edge or corner of the brush to work material into corners. Do not stuff the brush into these areas.
- For outside corners brush outward toward surface edge and then use up-stroke on adjacent surface to pick up runs or drips. For inside corners, brush upward from corner and then outward from the corner.
- Allow finishes to flow onto the wood and keep brushing to a minimum.

Cleanup

- Clean brushes immediately after use with the proper solvent. Do not allow finishing materials to dry in the bristles.
- Soak the brush in a can of the proper solvent.
- When the bristles are adequately saturated with solvent, work the solvent through the bristles with your fingers. Repeat until all of the material has been removed.
- Straighten and smooth bristles into original position.
- Dispose of used solvent properly.

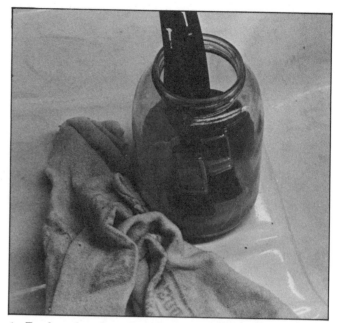

1. To clean brushes, first soak in proper solvent.

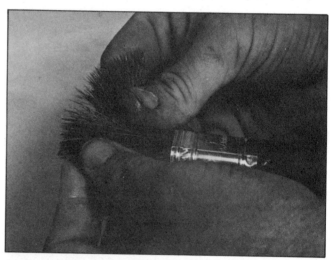

2. Work solvent through bristles.

3. Smooth bristles to original position.

Wood Sealers and Fillers

As a tree grows it retains a great deal of water in its trunk and limbs. When a tree is cut down, sawed into lumber, and allowed to dry, these deposits of water evaporate leaving spaces called wood pores. Every wood has pores. Fine-grained woods such as gumwood or pine have very small pores that are barely visible. Coarse-grained woods such as oak and wormy chestnut have large prominent pores.

Depending on the desired effect of the finish, these pores can be treated in a variety of ways. If you want a rough, natural look, nothing has to be done to the pores. Simply apply the finishing materials to the prepared or stained surface. The pores will remain open. If you want a smooth surface, however, the wood pores must be treated to prevent the finish materials from following the depressions of the pores. Fine- to medium-grained woods may only require a coat of sealer or liquid filler to effectively close the pores. Coarse-grained woods generally require a filler to provide a smooth surface.

Sealers are liquid finishing materials that will close the wood pores of fine-grained woods to prevent deep penetration of other finishing materials. Fillers are generally available in paste form and are used to fill the large open pores of coarse-grained woods. In some instances both fillers and sealers are used: a paste filler is used to close the pores followed with a coat of sealer to provide uniform penetration of both the wood and the filler.

Sealers

Sealers are often called liquid fillers or wash coats. Wood sealers have several important functions in wood finishing which are described below. They effectively close the small open pores of fine-grained woods. Many softwoods, such as fir, have special grain patterns that must be sealed. If not sealed, the grain pattern may be very pronounced and overwhelming.

For many years thinned shellac was the standard sealer for paint, varnish, lacquer, and shellac, but in recent years many new synthetic finishing materials have been introduced. Many of these products, however, will not adhere well to shellac. Carefully read the manufacturer's label to determine what can and cannot be used to seal the surface.

When to Use a Sealer Sealing can be useful at several points during the finishing process.

- A sealer can be applied directly to the bare wood surface. When used in this capacity, the sealer may be referred to as a wash coat or sanding

Sealer applied to bare oak.

sealer (previously described in the wood preparation chapter). Dried-out wood, wood with alternating areas of hardness and softness which differ in porosity, and softwoods will all quickly absorb a great deal of stain. By applying the sealer before staining, the surface can be sanded to a more uniform smoothness, varying areas of porosity can be made to absorb stain more uniformly, and stains will be prevented from penetrating soft, porous woods too deeply. A sealer is usually required when using an oil stain.

- A sealer can be applied over a stained surface. Depending on the solvent or chemicals used in the finishing material, the stain may bleed when placed in direct contact with the finish. The result is a muddy-looking finish. A sealer will provide a good barrier between two such incompatible

Sanding sealer applied to stained oak.

materials. The sealer, when lightly sanded, will provide a good surface for the finish to adhere to. A sealer should be applied to coarse-grained wood before filling because it facilitates easy wiping of the filler. A sealer will stiffen raised wood fibers after a water stain has been applied so they can be sanded off easily.

- A sealer can be applied after the filler. After sanding a coarse-grained wood surface that has been properly filled, a sealer can be applied to prevent the filler from bleeding through finish coats. Since the filler material differs from the surrounding wood surface in porosity, each material will absorb the finish to different degrees. A sealer will provide a uniform surface to ensure even absorption and a smoother finish.

Types of Sealers There are many sealers to consider. Several commercially prepared sealers are available at paint and hardware stores, and others can be easily prepared at home. The sealer you select should be determined by the type of finish you plan to use. Generally, the sealer is a thin coat of the final finish material.

For a shellac finish, thin shellac to a 1-pound-cut. This will penetrate and seal the wood very well. Shellac is generally sold in 4 or 5 pound cuts. To create a ½-pound-cut shellac, ideal for most sealing purposes, mix 1 part pure shellac to 3 or 4 parts denatured alcohol. A slightly thicker solution should be used when sealing a filler. Mix 1 part shellac to 2 or 3 parts denatured alcohol. Use white shellac for lighter woods and stains and orange shellac for darker woods and stains.

Shellac sealer can be used for varnish finishes as well. A varnish finish is tougher than shellac, but this does not hold true for sealers. In fact, shellac dries

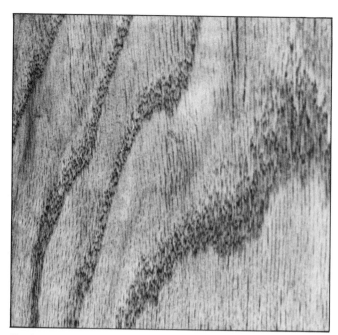

Sealer should be applied over a filled oak surface to create a surface that will accept stain or finish coats uniformly.

faster and is easier to sand than a varnish sealer. If you do not have shellac on hand or want to save the expense of purchasing two finishing materials, a good sealer for a varnish finish can be made by mixing 1 part natural varnish with 1 part pure turpentine or paint thinner. Synthetic varnishes cannot be reduced with turpentine or mineral spirits and do not require sealers. Read container labels carefully to be sure your varnish is natural and can be thinned.

For many lacquer finishes, you can use a shellac sealer or sanding sealer. If you have spraying equipment, a good lacquer sealer consisting of shellac sealer mixed with mixing lacquer can be sprayed on the stained surface. Use lacquer sealer only for lacquer finishes. Lacquer sealer can be brushed on, but spraying offers the best results.

If you plan to use polyurethane as the finish coat, the sealer should also be polyurethane, thinned with a solvent. Polyurethane thinners vary between brands, so read and follow the manufacturer's label carefully before preparing a sealer.

Commercial sealers are called sealers, penetrating sealers, sealer stains, or penetrating resins. Most of the finishes that are applied over sealers, such as shellac, varnish, or lacquer, are surface finishes—they simply lie on top of the wood surface. Many commercial sealers will penetrate the surface and harden to create a tough attractive surface. These sealers accentuate the wood's grain pattern and natural or stained color.

Many commercial sealers are available in wood tones. These sealers can serve as both stain and finish, or shellac or varnish can be applied over them. Commercial penetrating sealers are perfect for open

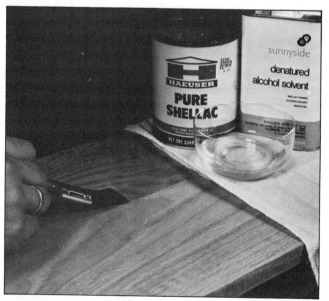

A 1-pound-cut shellac sealer applied to a filled, stained oak surface.

grained well-textured wood because the use of a wood filler is not necessary. They are equally effective on fine-grained woods.

Applying the Sealer Brush on sealers as you would any finishing material. Use straight, even-pressured strokes to apply a thin coat of sealer to the wood surface. Allow the sealer to flow from the brush. Coverage need not be heavy, only complete. Follow the manufacturer's instructions carefully. More than one coat of sealer may be required on very porous or dry woods. The sealer coat should dry dull, not shiny like the final finish coats. Allow each coat of sealer to dry thoroughly. Shellac sealers require 2-4 hours to dry, varnish sealers require 24 hours, lacquer sealers require 1-2 hours, sanding sealers generally require less than an hour, and polyurethane sealers require 3-6 hours. When completely dry, each sealer coat must be lightly sanded to ensure a strong bond between the sealer and subsequent finish coats.

Fillers

Oak, mahogany, and chestnut are woods with large open pores. Unless a rough, natural appearance is desired and a smooth finish is of no consequence, the pores of these woods must be filled. The pores can be filled by applying six, seven, or more coats of finish material, but this is both time-consuming and expensive. The resulting finish may be uneven and appear rippled or wavy. A more practical way to fill wood pores is with a paste or liquid filler. Some woods need more filler than others because of varying pore size and grain patterns.

Depending on the final effect desired, filler can be applied over bare wood, stained wood, or sealed wood. Fillers are available in common wood tones and a variety of colors. Some fillers are available in a neutral color. Tinting pigments can be added to the filler to closely match the natural or stained color of the wood. Many times the actual stain can be mixed with a neutral filler to make an exact match. Some fillers are transparent; others are opaque. For most finishing needs, try to use as transparent a filler as possible so the natural color and beauty of the wood will not be hidden.

Paste Fillers Paste fillers, the most common type, are generally used on open-pored, coarse-grained woods. They come in opaque or transparent form and usually have the consistency of thick paste which must be thinned prior to application. Paste fillers are available at most paint and hardware stores.

To properly fill large open pores, the filler must have several important qualities. It must adhere well to raw and stained wood surfaces, it must not shrink, crack or crumble when it dries, and it should dry hard and level with the surrounding wood surface. So far, the material that best meets these requirements is Silex. Silex is finely ground quartz that has no chemical action.

Coarse-textured woods such as oak have large clearly visible pores that should be filled.

Type of Filler for Common Woods

No Filler Needed	Thin Filler or Liquid Filler	Medium Filler	Heavy Filler
Aspen	Beech	Butternut	Ash
Basswood	Birch	Mahogany	Chestnut
Cedar	Cherry	Rosewood	Elm
Ebony	Gumwood	Walnut	Hickory
Fir	Maple		Oak
Hemlock	Pine		Teak
Pine	Sycamore		
Poplar			
Redwood			
Spruce			

The quartz powder is usually mixed with linseed oil and a drying agent to create a neutral-colored paste filler. Oil colors are added either by the manufacturer or the finisher to create colored fillers. Many fillers use materials other than Silex, but they are inferior.

When selecting a filler color, select one that resembles the actual color of the wood. A filler tends to be lighter when it dries, so a tone slightly darker than the wood should match the wood very closely. If you plan to mix your own wood filler color, first dilute the oil color with the proper solvent and then mix it with neutral filler. This tends to thin the filler slightly, but the filler must be thinned before application anyhow.

Many times a striking effect can be created by using a wood filler that is somewhat darker than the natural or stained wood color. This can accentuate the grain and add character to the wood. Generally, a lighter-colored filler gives wood an unnatural appearance.

How to Apply Wood Paste Filler Paste filler straight from the can is usually too thick to use properly, so it must be thinned. Most manufacturers recommend that turpentine, mineral spirits, or benzene be used. Follow the instructions on the filler container label. If you will be using stain to color a neutral paste filler, the stain will act as a thinning agent. Additional thinning, however, may be required. After thinning, the consistency should be that of a very thick cream. It should brush on without difficulty and should not lose any volume through evaporation. The filler should be stirred thoroughly several times during application.

The proper procedure for applying a wood paste filler is as follows:

1. The wood surface should be stained (if desired) and sealed prior to application of the filler.
2. Thin the paste filler to the recommended consistency and add the desired oil colors if you are using a neutral paste. Stir well.

3. Apply the wood filler generously with a stiff, wide, short-bristle brush. Neatness and evenness are not important, but thoroughly filling all the wood pores is. Work on only one small section at a time. The filler should be scrubbed into the wood pores and then brushed in the direction of the grain. The entire wood surface must be covered. If the filler appears thin in areas, particularly after scrubbing, reapply the filler in the direction of the grain. Stir the filler periodically during application.
4. Allow the filler to dry a few minutes until it begins to appear slightly dull. Do not allow the filler to dry completely, as removal will be very difficult.
5. Fold a coarse cloth, such as burlap, and vigorously rub the filler across the grain to work it deeply into the wood grain. Never wipe with the grain during this step. If you begin to wipe the filler too soon after application, some filler will be removed from the pores. The object is to remove filler only from the surface, not from the pores.
6. Immediately after this rough removal look closely at the wood pores. If the filled wood pores are not level with the surface, apply a thinned coat of paste filler to the surface and repeat the above steps.
7. Take a clean cloth or piece of burlap and rub in the same manner as described above to remove as much of the surface filler as possible. Follow this by lightly rubbing with a soft clean cloth in the direction of the grain to remove any remaining traces of the filler. Any filler remaining on the surface will alter wood color and grain pattern.

1. Apply thinned filler to wood.

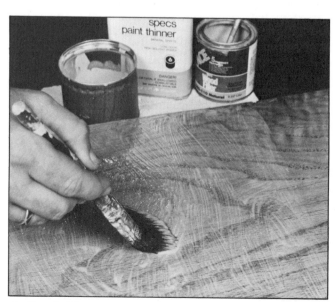

2. Scrub filler into all wood pores.

3. *Rub filler across grain with burlap.*

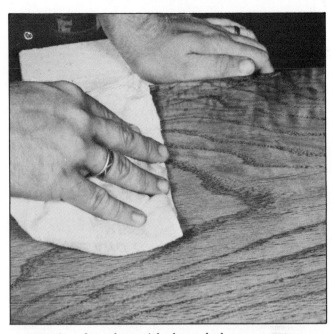

4. *Lightly rub surface with clean cloth.*

5. *Lightly sand the dried filler.*

6. *For additional smoothness use steel wool.*

8. Allow the filler to dry completely, at least 24 hours. Colored fillers generally require longer drying times.
9. Lightly sand the surface in the direction of the wood grain with a fine sandpaper. If you sand too hard or too deep, you will open more wood pores that will have to be filled.
10. Seal the filled surface properly.

Liquid Fillers Liquid fillers are essentially thick sanding sealers or thin paste fillers that serve the same purpose on close grain woods as the paste fillers do on open-grained woods. Because they contain very few solid silex particles, they can only be effectively used on closed-grained woods, such as birch, maple, and cherry. Although closed-grain woods do not need the amount of filling that open-grained woods do, liquid filler application helps to ensure uniform absorption of the finishing materials.

7. *The left side above has been filled, the right side has been left natural.*

Many materials can be used as liquid fillers: shellac, varnish, lacquer and sanding sealers, and thinned wood paste filler. The filler should be the same as the finish material. Shellac is the most popular liquid filler that is appropriate for most finishes, but some of the new synthetic varnishes will not adhere well to it. Use a liquid varnish filler for varnish finishes.

How to Apply Liquid Filler Liquid fillers are applied directly to a stained surface and allowed to dry thoroughly. They do not need to be wiped off. Since liquid fillers contain only a small amount of solid particles, they are transparent and can generally be applied over any color.

Liquid fillers are applied in the same manner as any regular finishing coat. The proper procedure is as follows:

1. Mix the liquid filler according to the manufacturer's instructions on the container label.
2. Brush a smooth, even coat of the filler over the surface, using straight strokes in the direction of the grain.
3. Allow the filler to completely dry, usually in a few hours. Varnish may require a longer drying time.
4. Sand lightly with a very fine abrasive paper. Try

Colored liquid filler was applied to this oak surface.

to remove the filler from the surface without removing any wood which would open new wood pores. Dust and clean the surface.

5. Repeat process for additional coats as necessary.

Popular Wood Finishes

In an earlier chapter you were advised to plan your finishing sequence in advance, taking into consideration the type of finish which would best serve the function of the wooden piece. By now you have spent considerable time and effort in preparing and staining the wood surface for an appropriate finish coat based on this function. But because of the wide range of finishing materials available, selecting the proper finish can be difficult.

A finish can do many things for a wood surface, but the primary purposes are to beautify and to protect. In general, you want a hard, beautiful surface. Each finish will create a different effect on the same type of wood. Clear finishes will accentuate and enhance the natural color and grain pattern of the wood. Some finishes will fill the open pores of coarse-grain woods while others will permit the pores to remain open. Either type of finish can be used depending on the effect that is desired and the function to be served.

Think carefully about the conditions the finished surface will be exposed to. Will the finish be subjected to drastic temperature changes, direct sunlight, moisture or water, or severe wear? Each finish reacts differently. Some are harder and more durable, some are water stain-resistant, and others are able to withstand temperature changes and direct sunlight. The function of the wood surface will determine which qualities the finish must have to effectively protect the surface from daily use.

Consider also the individual characteristics of each finish. Traditional finishes have been on the market for many years, but with the tremendous increase in do-it-yourself activity, many manufacturers have developed new chemical finishes that go on in one application, dry quickly, are less dangerous to use, and clean up quickly. Always read carefully the label on any finish. Most finishes are incompatible with at least one chemical that might be used in a sealer stain or filler. Use the finish only with the materials recommended on the label.

There are two basic types of finishes, penetrating finishes and surface coatings. Penetrating finishes, such as natural or synthetic oils and resins (linseed oil, lemon oil, Danish oil, penetrating resin, and the newer plastic finishes) are absorbed by the wood surface. The finish dries and hardens below the wood surface to give the wood a very natural appearance. They are generally used on modern or rustic pieces. These finishes are durable but will not take the punishment a surface coating will.

Surface coatings lie on the wood surface, providing a protective film that, when properly maintained, will resist most types of wear. Surface coatings include shellac, varnish, lacquer, polyurethane, paints, and enamels. The finish can be left in its natural glossy state, can be polished to create a high-gloss surface, or can be rubbed with very fine abrasives to provide a duller low-gloss sheen. Surface coatings are the most widely used finishes and are generally used on fine furniture or traditional pieces.

The Common Wood Finishes Chart outlines the basic advantages and disadvantages for each of the most popular wood finishes. A more detailed discussion will be presented for each finish later in the chapter.

Common Wood Finishes		
Finish	**Advantages**	**Disadvantages**
Shellac	• inexpensive surface coating • thins easily with alcohol • quick, easy application • relatively quick-drying • can be sanded and waxed • excellent first coat or sealer coat	• limited shelf life • not durable • liquids will soften and stain the finish • should be waxed
French Polishing	• inexpensive surface coating • requires little application time • durable with little maintenance required • excellent for finish repair • preferred finish for fine furniture	• can only be applied over specific stains (NGR or water-soluble) • difficult application • cannot be waxed

Varnish	• moderately expensive surface coating • extremely hard and durable • can be rubbed or polished to create several effects • excellent for surfaces subjected to hard use	• does not highlight grain pattern • cannot be applied over oil-base stains • somewhat difficult application • very long drying time; dust can be a problem • does not dry completely clear
Lacquer	• moderately expensive surface coating • easy application • extremely hard and durable • dries very quickly; dust generally not a problem • excellent for surfaces which require extra protection	• requires spray equipment • can only be applied over specific stains (NGR or water-soluble) • wood must be sealed
Polyurethane	• easy application • very durable, offers excellent protection • dries very quickly • excellent bare wood finish • stain and liquid resistant	• expensive surface coating • cannot be used over most fillers and sealers • tends to bubble • can only be thinned with special synthetic thinners
Penetrating Resin	• fast, easy application • good protection for penetrating finish • available in several colors • fillers and sealers not required • sanding and polishing not required • will highlight grain pattern well • excellent for natural look • easy maintenance	• expensive penetrating finish • cannot be used with stain fillers or sealers unless they are NGR or water-soluble
Rubbed Oil	• relatively inexpensive penetrating finish • easy application • water and stain resistant • excellent for natural finish, particularly on dark woods	• requires many coats • only fair durability • cannot be used over fillers and sealers • some types may be expensive
Paint/Enamel	• ranges from inexpensive to expensive • excellent coverup for stained or marred wood • good for poor-quality woods • available in many colors and sheens • most previous finish coats do not have to be stripped prior to application	• completely hides wood surface • not durable • must be sealed and filled • enamels have long drying time

Shellac

Shellac has long been a popular finishing material for both craftsmen and home finishers. The finish has a rich mellowness that will last for many years. It enhances the natural beauty and grain pattern of the wood by penetrating the surface slightly and drying to a clear, glossy finish. Shellac is very easy to apply, is durable, dries fast, and is uniquely beautiful. It will greatly intensify the natural color of both light and dark woods without obscuring the distinctive grain pattern. Shellac is also shock-resistant and will not crack when multiple coats are applied.

The popularity of shellac as a finish topcoat has diminished somewhat in recent years with the advent of the new synthetic finishes and sealers that duplicate many of shellac's desirable properties while eliminating the major disadvantages. A shellac finish can be easily damaged by water or alcohol. Liquids spilled on a shellac surface will discolor the finish. Liquids containing alcohol, such as alcoholic beverages and nail polish, will actually dissolve the finish. Shellac is not heatproof; heat will melt or blister the surface. Repair is next to impossible; therefore furniture that will be exposed to such conditions should not be finished with shellac. Table tops, dressers, and bar tops should be finished with another material. This problem can be minimized somewhat by applying a heavy coat of paste wax.

Shellac, despite its poor resistance to water and alcohol, is an excellent finish for most types of furniture. Shellac surfaces often require retouching because they tend to scratch more easily than other finishes, but because shellac is soluble in alcohol, this is a relatively simple procedure. Surface scratches and blemishes can be easily repaired by rubbing them lightly with a cloth dampened in alcohol or with a shellac stick.

Types of Shellac Shellac is an organic material made from the secretion of an insect found in Asia. The insect secretes a resin which slowly covers the entire insect, causing its death. The encrusted insects are harvested and crushed into tiny particles which are then heated over an open fire until melted. The melted residue is allowed to harden into thin sheets, then crushed into small powderlike flakes. Shellac manufacturers dissolve these flakes in denatured alcohol to create shellac.

The natural color of shellac is orange, but a bleaching agent can be added to the resin to make white shellac. Both white and orange shellac are transparent. Orange shellac is best suited for darker woods or stains, such as mahogany, walnut, redwood, or oak. If orange shellac is used on a lighter wood, it will discolor the surface slightly giving the wood an orange tint. This is not as apparent on a darker surface. Orange shellac can be used on knotty pine to give the wood an Early American appearance. Use white shellac on lighter stains or woods or when a blond finish is desired. White shellac will not appreciably change the color of the wood. White shellac does have a tendency to cloud when exposed to prolonged periods of moisture.

All shellac loses its quick-drying property and deteriorates when stored for an extended time, usually about six months. Some manufacturers date their containers, but to be safe, purchase only enough shellac to complete the project you are presently working on.

Preparing Shellac Shellac is always thinned with denatured alcohol before it can be applied to a wood surface. Shellac is commonly sold in several concentrations, called cuts, which indicate the amount of resinous flakes dissolved in one gallon of denatured alcohol. Common cuts are 3-pound-cut, 4-pound-cut, and 5-pound-cut. The cut of the shellac you buy will determine whether you will have to thin it.

The best way to achieve the clear luster of a quality shellac finish is to apply several thin coats rather than a single heavy coat. A 3-pound-cut shellac is considered the standard consistency for finishing; however, many craftsmen prefer building up a finish with multiple coats of 2- or 1-pound-cut-shellac. A good method is to apply several thin coats of 1- or 2-pound-cut shellac followed with a final coat of 3-pound-cut. The most economical way to make a 3- or 2-pound-cut is to thin 5-pound-cut shellac to the appropriate consistency.

All cuts of commercial shellac should be thinned before use. When thinned with alcohol, the shellac will flow onto the surface evenly. The thinner a shellac, the easier it is to brush. The following chart indicates the proportions of shellac and alcohol required to make specific cuts. Since the chart indicates parts of liquid volume, any convenient unit, such as pints or quarts, can be used.

Thinning Shellac to the Desired Cut			
Desired Cut	Original Cut	Parts Shellac	Parts Alcohol
1 pound	5 pound	1	2
1 pound	4 pound	1	2
1 pound	3 pound	3	4
2 pound	5 pound	1	1
2 pound	4 pound	4	3
2 pound	3 pound	5	2
3 pound	5 pound	2	1
3 pound	4 pound	1	2
3 pound	3 pound	—	—

It is not essential for the proportions to be precise. You can add shellac or alcohol as necessary to achieve the best working consistency. Use only denatured or grain alcohol for thinning and mix thoroughly.

Store the thinned shellac in tightly closed glass jars to avoid evaporation of the alcohol. Keep in mind the relatively short shelf life of shellac. Shellac will slowly become gummy as it ages. Date each container and keep it away from direct sunlight. Shake or stir the shellac well before using.

Applying Shellac Shellac has many uses as a finishing material. It is one of the best sealers for most finishes because it offers excellent surface adhesion. When using it as a sealer, never use a cut thicker than a 2-pound-cut. Try to apply it as thinly as possible. As a final finish, three to seven thin coats of shellac will produce a fine, durable protective film over the surface. The finish can then be rubbed a number of ways to produce varied effects. Shellac can also produce a finish called French polishing which is one of the most beautiful finishes possible. (This technique will be discussed in the next section.) The aniline dyes used in alcohol stains can also be dissolved in shellac. This produces a colored shellac or type of paint.

The standard shellac finish is not hard to apply. Several coats are required, but shellac is a quick-drying finish. The procedure for applying shellac to a wood surface is as follows:

1. Begin with 2-pound-cut shellac.

2. Apply shellac fast and efficiently.

1. Prepare the surface as described in previous chapters. Just prior to shellacking the surface remove all dust with a tack cloth. Position the piece so that you can finish the largest surface first.
2. Mix the shellac and pour into a wide mouth container, such as a glass jar or wide-mouth drinking glass. The first few coats should be 1- or 2-pound-cut followed with a final coat of 3- or 4-pound-cut. Novices generally achieve better results with the thinner cuts.
3. Select a soft 2-inch bristle brush for general work. A 3-inch brush can be used on large, flat surfaces. Fill the brush to capacity with shellac.
4. Shellac, because it dries quickly, must be applied fast and efficiently. Brush on the shellac with long uniform strokes in the direction of the grain. Overlap each stroke until the entire surface is covered. Should you miss a spot, do not attempt to touch it up. Just wait until the next coat.
5. For finishing turnings, legs, and other parts of the piece, use a smaller brush and just enough shellac to adequately cover the surface. Always

3. Use a smaller brush on turnings.

work around turnings and legs. Pick up any excess with a dry brush while the shellac is still wet.
6. When the entire surface is covered, allow about 2 to 4 hours for the shellac to dry thoroughly. (Shellac dries dust-free in about 15 minutes, but the finish is not ready for sanding and applying another coat.)
7. Lightly sand the entire surface with a very fine abrasive paper or steel wool, either 3/0 or 4/0. Flint paper, because it is inexpensive, should be used since shellac gums up the abrasive particles of most coatings. Position the abrasive in the palm of your hand and sand with long even strokes in the direction of the grain. Be careful not to sand through the finish to bare wood. This cannot be repaired. Sanding should remove any brush marks and provide a lightly scuffed surface that will allow the next coat to bond well with proceeding coat. Remove all sanding dust with tack cloth.

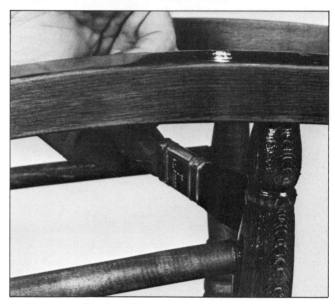

4. Lightly sand dried surface.

8. Apply several more coats of shellac to the surface in the manner described in the above paragraphs. Build up a finish of 4 to 7 coats. The last coat should be thicker than previous coats.

9. Sanding the final coat should be done with 4/0 steel wool after a minimum 24 hours drying time. Carefully clean the surface of all dust.

A shellac finish will benefit greatly from an application of paste wax. A buffed wax finish will highlight the shellac and protect the finish from water and alcohol. For more durable protection, the shellac-finished surface can be covered with a coat of thinned varnish rather than paste wax. Before applying paste wax or varnish, you can create several effects by omitting step 9 above and substituting one of the following techniques.

- A high-gloss finish and very smooth surface: allow the last coat of shellac to dry for 3 days. Rub the surface with pumice and raw linseed oil (described in a later chapter) in the direction of the grain with long uniform strokes. Clean residue carefully. A final sanding with rottenstone will create an even smoother surface. Polish with wax.
- A satin finish: allow the last coat of shellac to dry for 2 days. Rub the surface lightly with 3/0 steel wool until all the natural gloss of the shellac has been removed. Clean surface well with tack cloth. Polish with wax.
- A semidull finish: lightly sand the final coat of shellac with 4/0 steel wool, allowing some of the natural sheen to remain. Clean surface. Polish with wax.

French Polishing

Most period pieces are finished in this manner because French polishing creates a clear, smooth, velvety luster that enhances the grain pattern and highlights the natural wood color. The beauty of wood that has been French polished surpasses that of all other finishes. French polishing is not only beautiful, it is also a very practical finish. The finish will withstand wear and exposure for many years and can easily be repaired if the surface becomes damaged.

The technique for applying a French polish is not difficult, but the application requires time and rubbing that involves considerable physical effort. Several finishing materials, including shellac, alcohol and linseed oil, are used in French polishing. The finish is achieved by applying very thin coats of shellac to the wood surface to build up a glowing sheen, followed with several coats of boiled linseed oil.

French polishing is tedious, time-consuming hard work, but the results are well worth the effort. If you get tired, you can stop between coats and resume when tired muscles stop aching. Just lightly sand the last coat. The result is an amazingly beautiful finish that

5. *Rub final coat with steel wool.*

can add considerable value to an antique or fine piece of furniture.

In preparing a wood surface for French polishing consider the following factors:

- Use only water-soluble aniline dye stains beneath a French polish. The finish will not adhere to other stains.
- The surface must be as smooth as possible, so grain raising, sealing, and filling may be necessary. Closed-grained woods require sealing (the first thin shellac layer of a French polish will act as a sealer if properly applied). Open-grained woods must be filled and sealed.
- Sand and clean the surface with extreme care.

Prepare to apply a French polish by mixing 1-pound-cut shellac and folding a clean cloth into a pad.

1. Apply shellac to surface quickly.

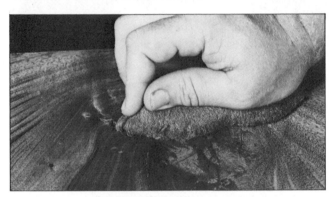

2. Rub dried surface with steel wool.

3. Add linseed oil to shellac.

4. Apply mixture with circular motion.

With the surface properly prepared, the following procedure should be used to apply a French polish.

1. Tightly wrap or fold a piece of lint-free cloth into a thick pad.
2. Pour 1-pound-cut shellac into a shallow open container. Some finishers add linseed oil to the shellac prior to application at the ratio of 1 tablespoon oil for each pint of alcohol in the cut shellac.
3. Dip the cloth pad into the shellac and apply to the surface with long, quick, light strokes in the direction of the grain. The surface of the pad should not be wrinkled. The secret to the deep luster and the success of the finish of French polish lies in the way it is applied and rubbed into the surface.
4. Allow this coat to dry thoroughly, approximately 1 hour.
5. Rub lightly with very fine steel wool or pumice and oil.
6. Apply several coats of shellac following steps 3, 4 and 5 carefully. A glowing sheen will have developed when enough coats have been applied.

5. Add linseed oil to surface.

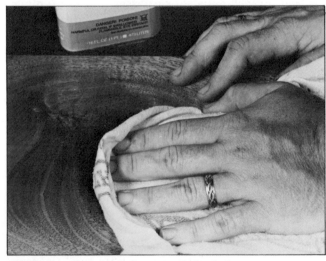

6. Wipe surface with denatured alcohol.

7. At this point mix several drops of boiled linseed oil with the cut shellac.

8. Apply the oil and shellac mixture with the pad, using a circular motion. It is important to begin this circular stroke before contacting the surface and to continue it onto the surface. Never stop rubbing once the pad is on the surface. Add an occasional drop or two of oil to the surface. Keep rubbing toward the edge and continue the motion until the entire pad is clear of the surface. Rub for 45-60 minutes. Allow to dry 24 hours.

9. Apply several coats in this manner, adding a few more drops of oil to the shellac for each successive coat. When the wood reaches the desired luster or gloss, stop rubbing. With each coat you will have to rub harder to keep the pad from sticking.

10. When the final coat has hardened (allow 1 week), take a soft cloth slightly dampened with denatured alcohol and pass it over the surface lightly to remove oil residue.

11. Apply paste wax to ensure a hard protective surface.

There are many types of varnish for many purposes.

Varnish

Varnish is considered the best all-purpose finish for the novice finisher because it is a beautiful clear finish with excellent hardness and durability. It is relatively easy to apply because of its flowing and leveling tendencies. One of the toughest finishes available, varnish is impervious to water, alcohol, and most liquids and will resist shock, abrasion, light, and heat better than most other finishes. Yet the finish dries transparent to highlight both grain pattern and natural color.

Varnish, more than any other finish, has seen many improvements in recent decades. Varnishes are now available in glossy, satin, or flat finishes, reducing the amount of final rubbing and polishing needed. Originally, varnish was made of natural oils and resins, drying agents, and turpentine. Although still available today, varnishes made of natural copal gums and linseed oil have been largely replaced by synthetic resins, such as polyurethane, alkyd, vinyl or phenolic. Synthetic resins provide varnish with additional durability and toughness, are easier to use, and, in some cases, dry faster than their natural resin counterparts.

There are many variations in varnish. It comes in many quantities, has a wide price range, and is available in glossy, satin, or flat finish. Consider several factors before selecting a varnish. Varnish is slow-drying, so try to select one that contains a drying agent. If you need additional hardness, try a polyurethane. Some varnishes have pigment added; will this affect the wood you are finishing?

Types of Varnish There are two basic types of varnish commonly used in furniture finishing: oil-based varnishes and synthetic-resin varnishes.

Oil varnishes have been used for centuries and are still available today. Natural resins and gums are suspended in tung oil or linseed oil. To reduce this mixture to a workable consistency, a thinner, such as turpentine or mineral spirits, is added. Oil varnishes also contain drying agents to lessen drying time once the varnish is applied.

As the thinning solvent evaporates and the oil dries, a solid film is left on the wood surface. This process requires a minimum of 24 hours, a time considerably longer than the drying time of synthetic-resin varnishes. The more oil used in an oil varnish, the longer it will take to dry.

The major disadvantages of a slow drying time are inconvenience, dust contamination, and improper drying. Building up a varnish finish can take several days. Because each coat dries so slowly, dust and other particles and even small insects often settle on the surface and become trapped in the finish. Try to work in as dust-free a room as possible. Sand each coat of varnish lightly with very fine sandpaper, making sure to clean up all sanding dust. The room should also have means to control temperature and humidity so the varnish will dry hard.

Oil varnishes, even with these shortcomings, are still used by the purist craftsman. When properly applied, they give a durable, beautiful finish, but for the most part, oil varnishes have been replaced by the synthetic-resin varnishes for most home-finishing needs.

Synthetic-resin varnishes are continually changing and improving. They have retained an oil-varnish resistance to water, alcohol, and mild acids but generally dry harder, exhibit better color retention with less yellowing, and will last much longer. Their greatest advantage is that they dry much faster than oil varnish. As stated earlier, there are several popular synthetic resins, but these resins are available in a variety of formulations. The result is a wide range of varnishes, one of which is likely to meet the specific requirements of your project.

Alkyd-based varnishes are suitable for finishing most types of furniture. They vary in color from clear to yellow and are generally the least expensive synthetic varnish. They are not extremely hard or durable, so they are best used on wood that will not be exposed to hard wear.

Vinyl-based varnishes are not as hard or as durable as some of the other synthetic-resin varnishes, but there are several advantages that make this product a popular finish. A vinyl-based varnish dries relatively fast, is exceptionally clear, and tends to have less of a darkening effect on the wood. Where retaining the natural wood color and enhancing grain pattern are important, vinyl-based varnish is a good choice.

Phenolic-based varnishes, sometimes called spar varnishes, are excellent for outdoor use but are of little value on indoor projects. Spar varnish contains very few drying agents, so the sun and wind will not dry it too quickly. It takes many days to dry thoroughly. It is very elastic, so it will not crack when exposed to drastic temperature changes. This quality prevents the varnish from becoming a hard surface. Spar varnish is extremely waterproof and will not whiten with age.

There are some new phenolic-based varnishes, called interior spar varnishes, that are excellent for indoor use on surfaces that are subjected to water or extreme moisture conditions. They will also dry hard enough for interior use.

Polyurethanes Polyurethane varnishes, the newest of the synthetic resins, are quickly replacing conventional varnishes. They are superior in many respects. Polyurethanes have exceptional hardness with the highest resistance to abrasion, moisture, and impact. They are easy to apply, dry very clear, and will not darken the wood. They dry dust-free in 30 minutes; another coat can be added after overnight drying.

The only true disadvantage is that the final coat cannot be hand rubbed; therefore, it should not be used on furniture that requires a hand-rubbed finish.

Polyurethane varnish can be applied over an existing varnish finish that has been cleaned and lightly sanded, over a raw wood surface, or over a stripped surface. Polyurethane cannot be applied over shellac or lacquer finishes or sealers. If you must seal raw wood before finishing, seal with polyurethane. Thin polyurethane varnishes only with the solvent recommended on the manufacturer's label. Use only fillers that are formulated for polyurethane finishes.

Never shake polyurethane prior to use. This action can cause bubbles. Several coats of polyurethane should be applied to build up a finish that offers maximum protection and beauty. Sand each coat to ensure proper adhesion of the next coat. Polyurethanes do not bond well chemically, so each coat must be lightly sanded to create a good mechanical bond. The polyurethane finish will lift from any area that was not sanded properly. There are a couple of polyurethane varnishes on the market that do not require sanding between coats if the next coat is applied within a certain time period. Follow all label instructions closely for drying times and recoating intervals.

Polyurethanes, like most synthetic resin varnishes, come in three basic finish styles. Each style is based on the degree of shine the finished surface will have. All natural resin and oil varnishes have a glossy finish. The only way to reduce this very high mirrorlike shine is to rub the surface with pumice and oil or rottenstone. The synthetics are available in glossy, satin, or flat finishes. A satin or semigloss finish will tone down the shine somewhat and reduce the reflective effect to a degree. Flat finishes have no sheen and are dull in appearance.

Preparation Sand, smooth, and stain the wood surface as you would for any other finish. The wood should be sealed with varnish or shellac unless you plan to use a polyurethane. Polyurethane will only bond with a sealer of the same material. Do not apply varnish over an oil stain.

Applying a varnish stain requires a controlled environment. The room must be dust-free and dry. Humidity can cause the varnish to dry too slowly or cloud. The temperature should remain a constant 70° to ensure proper flow from the brush during application and uniform, proper drying. If temperatures are too warm, the varnish may run. If they are too cool, the varnish will not spread properly which may cause blistering. The work area should be well ventilated without a draft. Earlier in the chapter, the importance of a dust-free environment was stressed. To help accomplish this, wet the floor or sprinkle with wet sawdust, place only fresh newspaper over the work area, do all sanding in a separate, enclosed area, and wear clothing that will not shed dust or lint.

When cleaning the surface prior to varnishing or when cleaning a sanded coat prior to the application of the next coat, wipe the surface with a tack cloth to remove any particles of dust or dirt. This sticky pad can be purchased from a paint or hardware store. To make your own, soak an old cotton handkerchief or similar cloth in warm water, wring it out, splash with turpentine, and pour a little varnish over the surface. Force all the moisture out of the cloth by squeezing it tightly and allow to dry a few hours. The rag should be tacky not wet. Store in an airtight container.

Thinning Varnish A few varnishes are ready to use straight from the can. Others require thinning. If you plan to use a varnish sealer before applying the finish coats, you will have to thin the varnish. Thinning a varnish can also help achieve a consistency that is easier to brush on. Once you begin applying the finish, the varnish will have to be thinned periodically to keep the material at a uniform consistency. A thinner first coat will also create a better bond between the sealer and finish.

Thinning is generally done with either turpentine or mineral spirits, although some synthetic resin varnish formulations may require a special synthetic solvent. Read the manufacturer's directions on the container label for proper thinning instructions. Varnish is generally thinned with a solvent at a ratio ranging from 5:1 to 7:1, depending on the consistency desired. Never mix two kinds of varnish together.

When you add a thinning solvent to a varnish or when you prepare to open the can, never shake the can. Shaking or even vigorous stirring can cause bubbles that will be very difficult to brush out. Stir the varnish slowly for several strokes. Allow the varnish to stand a few minutes so any trapped bubbles can work their way to the surface and escape. Repeat the procedure and pour the varnish carefully into a varnish cup or shallow pan. Bubbles can be minimized further by using a strike wire across the top of the container to remove excess varnish from the brush as drawing the loaded brush across the curved lip of the can will cause bubbles. Careful brushing will also prevent bubbles.

Applying Varnish Varnish can be applied by brushing or with a pad. Brushing is the more accepted and effective technique. A varnish brush should be exceptionally clean and of excellent quality. A good brush will make a noticeable difference. A 2-inch natural bristle brush is good for most surfaces, but a 3-inch brush can be used on large, flat surfaces. Clean new brushes in turpentine before using them for the first time.

Prepare a brush for use by dipping it in varnish and working it back and forth rapidly to evenly distribute the varnish through the bristles.

Try to position the piece so that the surface you are varnishing is horizontal. Varnish tends to run, so achieving an even coat on a vertical surface may be difficult.

The actual application sequence of varnish is similar to other finishes; however, certain characteristics of the varnish require a unique brushing method. The procedure for brushing varnish over a wood surface is as follows:

1. Prepare the wood surface as you would for any finish. Seal the surface with the sealer recommended on the varnish container label. Allow the sealer to dry completely. Sand lightly and remove all dust.

2. Fill the brush by dipping it into the varnish about one third of the bristle length. Flow the varnish onto the surface gently by holding the brush at a 45 degree angle with the bristles just touching the surface. Do not bend the bristles. Use long light, even strokes parallel to the grain. Apply liberally with a minimum number of strokes. Try to go from one end to the other with one stroke. If this is impossible, start in the middle of the surface and stroke toward the edge. Refill the brush and, starting at the center again, stroke to the

1. Flow varnish onto the surface in direction of the grain.

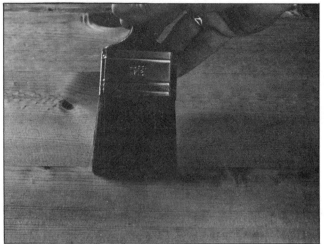

2. Brush across the grain to ensure thorough even coverage.

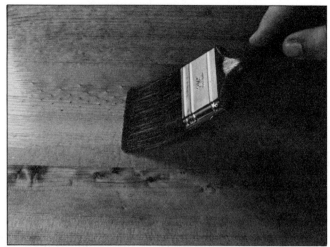

3. Tip off by brushing in the direction of grain with a nearly dry brush.

opposite edge. This method will help eliminate thick deposits of varnish at the edges. Always work parallel to the grain.

3. Thin the varnish as necessary to ensure uniform consistency. Cover the can loosely when not in use.

4. Immediately after covering the surface with strokes parallel to the grain, use strokes across the grain to ensure thorough coverage in the appropriate method as described in step 2.

5. Using a strike wire, remove all excess varnish from the brush. The coat is finished by tipping off. The bristle ends of a nearly dry brush should be lightly drawn across the surface in strokes parallel to the grain. This step will eliminate visible brush strokes, minimize bubbles, and more evenly and smoothly distribute the varnish over the surface. Tip the entire surface. Do not be concerned with small brush marks. These will flow into the surrounding surface as the varnish dries.

6. Brush lengthwise on legs with flat surfaces and around turnings. Tip halfway up and halfway down. Delicate carvings should be thoroughly covered with varnish. A dry brush can then be used to remove the pools of varnish that collect in the depressions or grooves of the carving.

7. Allow the varnish to dry at least overnight, if not longer. When you can touch the surface without leaving a fingerprint, you can recoat. After applying the first coat examine the surface closely as the varnish dries. Should dust or other particles land on the finished surface, they can be taken off with a pick stick. A pick stick is actually a tool with a sharp point that can be used to remove the particle without marring the surface. A toothpick or an artist's brush dipped in varnish will work fine. Try to remove all particles while the varnish is wet. Varnish will dry dustproof in about one hour.

8. When the initial coat of varnish is completely dry, sand the surface lightly with a fine grade of abrasive paper or steel wool. Work with light pressure in the direction of the grain. This will level any high spots and ensure better adhesion of the next coat. The abrasive can be used wet or dry. Sand until you achieve a satin look.

9. Clean the surface carefully and thoroughly after sanding.

10. Apply as many coats of varnish as needed. These additional coats are applied in the same manner as the first. Watch the drying times of successive coats carefully. If the varnish is not given sufficient time to dry, sanding may tear away parts of the finish. Allow the first coat to dry approximately 24 hours, the second, 48 hours, and the final coat up to 3 days.

11. The last coat does not require sanding; it will be rubbed and polished as explained in a later chapter. The varnish surface can be rubbed to a glossy or satin finish.

12. When you are through with a varnishing brush, work the bristles in benzene or turpentine until all of the varnish is dissolved, wipe clean, and store. If you use paint thinner to clean the brush, wash the brush with benzene prior to storage.

Problems Several problems can arise with a varnish finish, but most can be prevented quite easily. Listed below are several common varnishing problems and their respective solutions.

- Dust: This problem and ways to minimize it were discussed earlier in this section.
- Bubbles: If you stir or brush the varnish too vigorously, bubbles can form. When the varnish dries, these bubbles pop, causing a crater to form. Removing such craters is difficult.
- Pinholes: If the varnish is applied over a surface that is not entirely dry, pinholes can appear as the varnish dries. Pinholes can also form if a cheap

4. *Remove dust or lint.*

5. *Lightly sand dried surface.*

6. *Recoat in same manner.*

7. *Rub surface to desired gloss.*

A varnished surface is very hard, durable, and beautiful. It is an excellent finish to use on children's furniture.

thinner is used or if the thinner was not properly mixed with the varnish.

- Runs: Too much varnish on a surface will cause runs. So will very humid conditions. The best way to avoid runs is to position the piece, if possible, so that you are always working on a horizontal surface.
- Cloudiness: Most cloudiness is caused by impurities on a used paintbrush. Paint and some finishing materials that have become trapped in the bristles of your brush will mix with the clear varnish and solvent to create a slightly opaque finish. Note: polyurethane varnish and shellac are not compatible materials. If you apply polyurethane over a shellac sealer, the finish is likely to cloud.
- Brush Marks: Brush marks can be avoided by brushing in the manner described. Brush marks generally result from too small a brush or too much brushing.
- Chipping or Cracking: If you use an old varnish, it may dry brittle and crack or chip. If you use one type of varnish over another, one type may shrink more during drying than the other. This can also cause cracking.
- Missed Areas of Coverage: Working in good light, preferably natural, will reveal dry spots and other flaws before the varnish dries. They can easily be fixed while the varnish is wet.

Lacquer

In recent years, lacquer has replaced varnish and shellac as a finishing material in most commercial furniture manufacturing. Professional craftsmen also are using lacquer more often for custom finishing. There is excellent reason for such an increase in popularity. Lacquer dries to a hard, durable finish that is able to withstand moisture, heat, alcohol, and some acids. It has the fastest drying time of all wood-finishing materials and offers a thin, clear surface that highlights both color and natural wood grain. Lacquer has less tendency to darken the wood than other finishes.

But lacquer has one major disadvantage for the home refinisher that often makes using it impractical. Lacquer must be sprayed to achieve a quality finish. Good lacquers contain acetone which evaporates almost immediately when applied in a thin coat. Lacquers are dry to the touch in only a few seconds. Brushing such lacquers is nearly impossible because one stroke is almost dry before the next is applied. This will cause serious overlap marks and an uneven finish, particularly for the novice.

Since commercial manufacturers and professional craftsmen have quality spray equipment, lacquer is very practical and economical because a durable, beautiful finish can be applied in a matter of hours. Shellac application requires days; varnish, a week or more. But for the home finisher, purchasing the appropriate spray equipment can be expensive and using the equipment properly requires several hours of practice.

Several manufacturers have mixed special agents with their lacquers to slow down the drying process. These lacquers are intended to be applied with a brush. The drying time is still quite rapid, however, and such lacquers require careful brushing. Brushing lacquers are not as readily available as spraying or regular lacquers. Some lacquers are also available in aerosol form.

Lacquer cannot be mixed at home because it contains many synthetic materials in a complex chemical composition. Lacquer's basic ingredients are nitrocellulose resins or gums, softeners, thinners, and a solvent, usually acetone. Acetone, in addition to evaporating quickly, is also a strong, highly volatile solvent that is not compatible with the chemicals used in many sealers, stains, and fillers. Be sure to use lacquer only with the finishing materials recommended on the container. Shellac is generally a good sealer to use beneath a lacquer finish.

Wood should be sealed prior to lacquering. The strong solvent in lacquer may cause the natural dyes of the wood to bleed through the finish, particularly the darker woods such as mahogany and ebony. Shellac or a lacquer sanding sealer can be used to seal a natural surface, stained surface, or filled surface.

Types of Lacquer There is a wide variety of natural and synthetic lacquers available. These types of lacquer can be subdivided into two basic categories for the homeowner, spraying lacquers and brushing lacquers. The only difference between them is drying time. Both are available in flat or gloss finishes.

The primary types of lacquer are:
- Clear gloss lacquer—dries hard to a high-gloss finish. Very durable. Can be rubbed. Can be used on all types of furniture and wood products.
- Flat lacquer—same as clear gloss lacquer except that it dries to a dull, flat finish. Gives rubbed appearance without the smoothness or the work.
- Lacquer enamels—colored lacquers that are generally available in aerosol cans. Dries to a hard, durable surface. Available in flat, gloss, or satin finish.
- Acrylics—extremely durable finish that provides a tough, clear finish that is highly resistant to water, alcohol, and some chemicals.

Spraying lacquers for household finishing projects are simply smaller quantities of the lacquer used by furniture manufacturing companies. Most of these lacquers are ready for spraying straight from the container. Spraying generally requires four to six coats of lacquer, but the application time is not very long because of the rapid drying. Spray lacquers are also available in aerosol cans, but these are not effective or efficient for most home-finishing needs.

Spray equipment is a good investment if you plan to do a number of finishing projects each year and if you have an effective ventilating system.

If spraying is not feasible, several manufacturers have developed brushing lacquers. Brushing lacquers, although not available in as many varieties as spraying lacquers, are now widely available at most large paint and hardware stores. They have a slower drying time which makes brush application possible, but they do not perform as well as spraying lacquers because of the agents added to slow the drying process. They must be flowed on with very little brushing action. Usually two or three coats are adequate.

Brushing lacquers are suitable for small objects. Spraying lacquers work best on large objects with broad flat surfaces as spray application will not leave brush marks. Brushing lacquers can be sprayed also with good results, but do not try brushing spray lacquers.

Lacquer thinner is used to thin spraying and brushing lacquers and to clean up spray equipment or brushes. Use only the thinner recommended by the lacquer manufacturer.

1. *Fill the brush by dipping into lacquer one third the bristle length.*

2. *Squeeze off excess lacquer against the side of the container, rather than the lip.*

3. *Flow lacquer onto surface rapidly, holding brush at a 45-degree angle.*

4. *Brush around turnings. Excess lacquer in the depressions can be removed with cotton swabs.*

Applying Lacquer There are two ways to apply lacquer, by brushing or by spraying. Since brushing does not require expensive elaborate equipment, it is the technique most home finishers will use. Follow these steps to apply brushing lacquer:

1. Prepare and smooth the surface properly. Stain and fill the wood if necessary. Seal with shellac or lacquer sealer to seal stain or natural color and provide good surface for finish. Try to position each surface horizontally.

2. Pour lacquer into clean container. Use a large brush (2-3 inches) to keep brush marks to a minimum. Fill the brush; squeeze off excess against the side of the container (do not drag across rim lip).

3. Holding the brush at a 45 degree angle, allow the lacquer to flow from the brush to the surface with rapid, even strokes. Do not work the brush back and forth across the surface. Work in the direction of the grain; turn the brush and stroke the other way until the brush needs refilling. Carry each stroke as far as possible. Overlap strokes only slightly.

4. If the lacquer is not flowing easily, add a little of the proper thinner.

5. For long surfaces, always work from the ends to the center, blending two opposite strokes in the center. For turned or uneven surfaces avoid allowing the lacquer to pool in depressions or grooves. Apply lacquer and tip off with a nearly dry brush.

6. Cover entire surface and allow to dry for approximately 2 hours.

7. Sanding is not necessary between coats unless roughness is apparent. Additional coats will bond chemically with the initial coat.

5. Rub the final coat to the desired gloss.

8. Apply other coats as desired. If you plan on using a flat finish, all undercoats should be clear gloss. Only the top coat needs to be flat lacquer.

9. Rub final coat to desired finish.

Spraying lacquer is easier and more effective than brushing provided you have the proper equipment and necessary experience. Please review the section on spray finishing in a previous chapter. Follow these steps to apply spraying lacquer:

1. Prepare the surface as you would for brushing.

2. Use from 20 to 40 pounds of pressure. The lower the pressure, the thinner the lacquer and the more coats needed. Thin the lacquer as suggested by the manufacturer.

3. Test the equipment and lacquer by spraying several test patterns. The secret to a quality spray finish is properly functioning equipment.

4. The best pattern for lacquer is an oval shape, wet and solid in the middle blending out to a fine spray around the edges.

5. Carefully following a definite sequence, begin spraying the project. Cover the entire surface. Sanding is not necessary.

6. Apply as many coats as you feel necessary.

7. Rub final coat to desired finish.

As mentioned earlier in this section, lacquer is also available in aerosol cans. Although not as efficient as spraying or brushing, aerosol application offers great convenience to the home finisher. This method of application should be used only for small surfaces or touch-up. Follow these steps to apply lacquer in aerosol cans:

1. Shake can well. Follow manufacturer's instructions.

2. Depress spray valve to release lacquer.

3. Hold can approximately 12 inches from the surface. Keep this distance uniform during the entire spraying operation.

4. Spray back and forth in a slow, even manner until entire surface is covered.

Oil Finishes

A rubbed oil finish is a fine traditional finishing method that dates back to colonial America. An oil finish produces a rich, mellow color and natural beauty that many craftsmen feel is superior to all other finishes. It has long been the most popular finish for antique woods, particularly close-grained hardwoods. The finish, when applied properly, is able to withstand heat, water, and stains, and is quite durable. A rubbed oil finish does not require waxing.

Oil penetrates deeply into the wood surface to create a hard layer in the wood itself. For this reason oil can only be applied over bare or stained wood. Since the beauty of an oil finish depends entirely on penetration, the oil cannot be applied over sealers or fillers that may impede penetration. Some woods tend to overdarken when an oil finish is applied. For example, walnut may turn black. Test the oil first on a concealed area.

In recent years, modern synthetic finishes and penetrating resins have all but replaced rubbed oil finishes. Oil finishes require time and hard work. The actual finishing process may take a year or longer. Fortunately, the piece can be used during much of this time. Actual application requires exhaustive rubbing to help drive the oil deep into the wood. Many coats are required to build up a durable, protective finish. But, if you are willing to devote hours of hard work to the finish, rubbed oil will create a very beautiful surface.

Applying an Oil Finish Application of an oil finish is basically simple; it just requires time and a great deal of hard-pressure rubbing. You will have to be patient. Oil has a very long drying time, and successive coats cannot be applied before the previous coat has dried thoroughly. Follow these steps:

1. Be certain that any bare wood surface is completely free of any previous finishing materials, dust, or grease. Do not seal or fill the wood.

2. Use only boiled linseed oil; not raw linseed oil. Linseed oil is made by crushing flaxseed into a rough oil. The raw oil will not dry, but when it is processed by either boiling or adding driers, it develops much better drying characteristics. Even boiled linseed oil remains slightly tacky, particularly in hot weather.

3. Mix approximately 3 parts boiled linseed oil with 1 part turpentine or mineral spirits. (Precise measurements are not crucial.) Heat this mixture slightly in a double boiler to improve penetration of the oil.

4. Apply the mixture to a specific limited area of the surface with a clean, saturated lint-free rag. Rub the oil into the surface for 15-20 minutes or until the surface will no longer absorb the oil. Begin with flat surfaces.

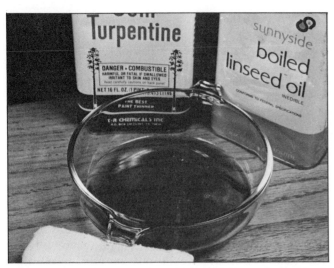

1. An oil finish must use only boiled linseed oil mixed with turpentine.

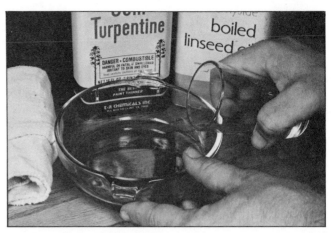

2. Mix proper proportions.

5. Try not to flood grooves and carvings, so the oil does not settle in the depressions and remain tacky. Cool oil should be used on turnings and carvings.

6. All concealed wood and underside surfaces must be oiled as well to avoid warping.

7. Rub the surface vigorously with a clean lint-free rag for another 20 minutes or until all excess oil is removed (this is accomplished when you can press your hand to the surface and not pick up any trace of oil).

3. Apply mixture with clean rag.

8. Allow at least 1 day for the initial coat to dry completely.

9. From 8 to 20 coats of oil will be needed to achieve the luster you desire. You can stop when the wood looks the way you want it to. The drying time between coats varies. Remember that the previous coat must be absolutely dry before you can continue, or subsequent coats will become sticky. The more coats you apply, the longer the drying time between coats.

10. The following schedule will allow you to build up a warm, glowing finish in less than a year; apply

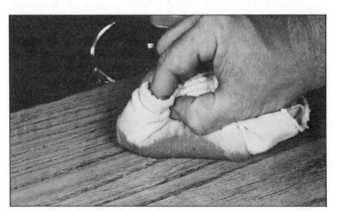

4. Rub oil into surface.

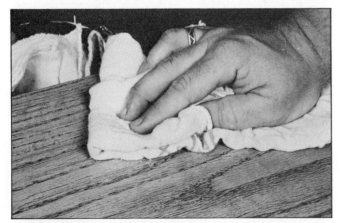

5. Rub surface with clean rag.

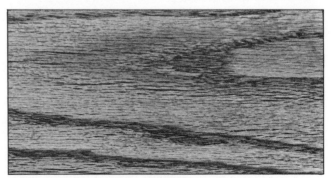

6. A beautiful, natural oil finish.

2 more coats at 2 or 3 day intervals, apply 1 coat each week for 1 month and 1 coat each month for the rest of the year or until a soft luster is accomplished. A boiled linseed oil finish must be renewed 2 or 3 times each year by applying a coat of oil as described above.

In recent years manufacturers have developed oil finishes that produce the rich luster of a boiled linseed oil finish without all the hard effort. Generally, only two to four coats are needed. Modern oil finishes are considerably more expensive, but they do offer the following advantages:

- They penetrate deeply and seal wood pores, making repair and renewing easy.
- They dry quickly and require less applications than linseed oil.
- They accentuate the natural wood beauty and closely resemble the fine finish created by many hours of rubbing a linseed oil finish.
- They tend to soften less under warm conditions.

Apply modern oil finishes as directed on the manufacturer's label.

Penetrating Resin Finishes

Most of the popular finishing materials such as shellac, varnish, lacquer, and polyurethane are surface finishes, meaning that they beautify and protect the wood by building up a strong glasslike film on top of the wood surface. One of the newest finish materials, however, penetrates the wood surface deeply and hardens to create a durable but flexible finish just beneath the actual surface.

This finishing material is most commonly called penetrating resin but is known by several other names as well, including penetrating finish, Danish oil, penetrating oil finish, penetrating wood sealer, and penetrating resin-oil finish.

A penetrating resin finish is a type of oil finish. It can be a combination of several materials but is generally a base of synthetic alkyd resins and/or tung oil to which a sealer stain has been added. Some penetrating resins contain varnish or plastics. Others contain pigments and are available in many wood-tone shades.

Penetrating resins are ideally suited to the finisher without much experience because they are the easiest finish to apply. They are brushed or wiped on a wood surface, allowed to penetrate and then the excess is wiped away. Do not be concerned with brush or overlap marks. Penetrating resin finishes dry by evaporation.

The synthetic resins or tung oil of a penetrating resin are absorbed deeply into the wood pores where they harden to create a hard subsurface that is impervious to water, heat, alcohol, most chemicals, and scratches. Penetrating resins resist wear better than most other finishes because the protective coat actually extends below the wood surface to create a harder wood. Penetrating resins also resist rot-causing fungi and insects. Wood finished with a penetrating resin also has increased dimensional stability which greatly reduces shrinkage and warping.

Perhaps the greatest advantage to using a penetrating resin finish is that, unlike the surface finishes, the natural texture of the wood grain is not covered. You can feel the true rich texture of an open-grained wood when you run your hand across the wood surface. This finishing material is the best choice when a natural appearance and feel is desired. Penetrating finishes are also being used more frequently on antiques where a fine wood can be greatly enhanced (and protected) by the finish. Penetrating resins do have one serious disadvantage. Stripping a penetrating resin properly can be nearly impossible because of the finish's deep penetrating qualities.

Hard open-grained woods, such as oak, teak, chestnut, mahogany, or walnut, benefit most from a penetrating resin finish. Some woods, particularly teak and rosewood, have oily resinous deposits that make finishing with materials other than penetrating resins very difficult. Penetrating resins enhance woods that possess a rich natural character but are not as striking when used on close-grained woods with little noticeable grain pattern.

Penetrating resins can only be applied to bare wood or wood stained with a water base or NGR stain. Staining over a stripped surface is not recommended because the wood pores are often clogged with the previous finishing materials, and this will adversely affect penetration of the resins and/or oils. Fillers and sealers are not necessary for a penetrating resin finish. Do not use other finishing materials with a penetrating resin.

Because penetrating resin is absorbed so deeply into the wood pores, the finish will not have a smooth glossy shine like the surface finishes. A satin finish can be achieved, however, by buffing, or if additional luster is desired, the surface can be waxed and polished. If you desire a smooth surface, several coats can be applied to fill the coarse open wood pores, but then the natural finish is eliminated. Since there is no surface film with a penetrating resin, scratches are virtually eliminated. Resanding and renewing the surface is unnecessary.

Should a penetrating resin finish become damaged, repair is very simple. Lightly scuff the surface with steel wool and add another coat of penetrating resin. This will repair most superficial damages.

A clear penetrating oil will darken the wood somewhat and highlight the grain considerably. This finish tends to darken darker woods more than lighter ones. The darkening effect is usually not objectionable be-

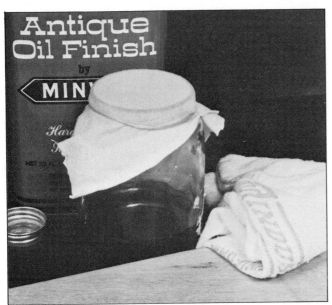

1. *Strain penetrating resin through nylon before applying to remove impurities and sediment.*

2. *Apply the resin liberally with a brush to totally saturate the surface.*

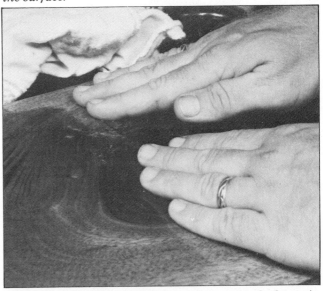

3. *Rub your hands around on surface to work the resin further into the wood pores.*

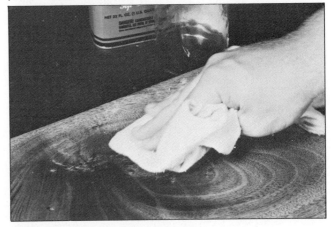

4. *Remove excess with clean rag.*

cause the darkness in no way obscures grain pattern or texture.

Applying Penetrating Resin Penetrating resin finishes are easy to apply. Prepare a bare wood surface as you would for any other finish. Do not seal or fill the surface; the penetrating resin itself will serve both of these functions. Be sure to remove all dust and dirt from the surface.

1. Strain the penetrating resin by pouring the finish through an old nylon stocking into a clean container.
2. Try to position the piece so that you are always working on a horizontal surface. This will make application much easier and penetration much deeper.
3. Apply the penetrating resin liberally with a clean lint-free cloth or brush. Many home finishers pour the material onto the surface and then work it around with a brush or rag. Do not be concerned with brush marks or runs at this point. Just totally saturate the surface using a light circular motion.
4. Keep applying the finish until it is no longer absorbed by the wood. Keep the surface wet for 30 minutes (or the time recommended by the manufacturer) to ensure good penetration. Add more resin when the surface begins to dull. When the surface is sufficiently wet, rub your hands around on the surface to warm the resin and work it into the wood pores.
5. When you are certain that the wood is well saturated, begin removing the excess resin by wiping the surface with a clean lint-free cloth. Use long moderate-pressure strokes in the direction of the wood grain. The surface should appear dull and dry looking when sufficiently wiped clean.

6. Allow the finish to dry and harden for 24 hours (some types may require less time; see the manufacturer's instructions).

7. Sanding between coats is not necessary; however, lightly rubbing the surface with a fine steel wool between coats can remove bubbles, provide a better surface for the second coat to adhere to, and can expose more wood pores to improve penetration of the second coat. Light sanding may increase luster slightly. Clean the surface with a tack rag.

8. Generally, two coats will provide a beautiful, durable surface. Porous woods may benefit from a third coat. A third coat will also add hardness and durability to surfaces that will be exposed to hard wear. Apply additional coats of penetrating resin until the wood no longer accepts the finish. (Most woods will benefit little from more than 3 coats.)

9. Apply additional coats in the same manner as the initial coat. Allow successive coats to dry 24 hours (longer in humid conditions).

10. If you are finishing a darker wood like walnut or mahogany, you can use crocus cloth instead of lint-free cloths when wiping off excess resin. The crocus cloth will leave the surface extremely smooth and impart a slight reddish tint to the finish. This generally enhances dark wood colors.

11. After the final coat is dry, you can polish the surface to a variety of lusters, add a final coat of wax or possibly varnish, or complete the finishing with only a light sanding if you prefer the natural appearance.

5. Lightly rub hardened surface with fine steel wool.

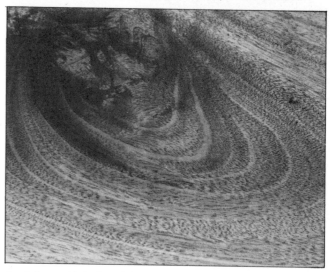

6. A beautiful, durable surface is created when resin is properly applied.

Paints and Enamels

Most of the finishes discussed in previous sections of this chapter become a clear transparent film when they dry on a wood surface. But there are times when covering the surface with an opaque finish of paint or enamel is desirable or necessary.

Several woods have uninteresting, plain grain patterns that will not be accentuated by a stain or finish. Previously finished wood furniture may have been damaged, requiring extensive repair with wood filling compounds. Some new furniture is constructed of low grade lumber or several types of lumber that will not have a uniform appearance when stained. Occasionally you may want to match a piece of furniture to surrounding furniture or a particular room decor. In each of these cases, a paint or enamel finish will hide the wood's natural characteristics beneath a protective, colorful opaque film.

Paint and enamels have many common characteristics and are used for the same purposes, but they are two separate materials. Paints are generally pigments dispersed in an oil vehicle to which driers and a thinner are added. Enamels are actually colored varnishes. Pigments are ground into varnish rather than oil. Most modern enamels have synthetic bases like those in varnish. Alkyd enamels are most popular. Polyurethane enamels offer extra hardness and protection. Driers and thinners are added to hasten drying and improve brushing qualities.

Enamels are more popular than paint for finishing furniture because they are harder, last longer, and can be polished. Enamels also clean easier than paints, usually just by washing the surface with soap and water. Water-soluble, latex or acrylic paints and enamels should not be used on furniture.

Paints and enamels are available in a wide variety of colors. Most reputable paint and hardware stores can custom-mix a color quite easily. You can mix your own colors as well, but with the wide range of standard and custom colors available, this is seldom necessary.

1. *Undercoat before applying enamel.*

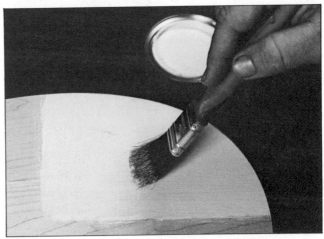

2. *Vigorously apply undercoat.*

3. *Brush in all directions to ensure thorough coverage.*

4. *Tip off excess undercoat with a nearly dry brush.*

Never mix different brands or kinds of paints and enamels. Paints and enamels are available in a gloss, semigloss, or flat finish. Glossy enamels are the most durable, but they also highlight surface irregularities to a greater degree.

Most paints and enamels come ready to use. If you plan to apply several coats (generally two to four coats are adequate), the first coat can be thinned slightly according to the manufacturer's recommendations. Like varnishes, enamels and oil-based paints require at least 24 hours to dry. There are several new quick-drying enamels that dry in about four hours. Enamels are also available in aerosol cans, but these are not appropriate for fine furniture.

Applying Paints or Enamels Prepare the surface as you would for any other finish. A paint or enamel finish must be as smooth as possible. If you plan to refinish with a paint or enamel, the existing finish, provided it is in good condition (no peeling or cracking) does not have to be stripped unless it is a waxed, rubbed oil, or polyurethane finish. Lightly sand the existing finish to provide a surface that the paint or enamel can adhere to properly.

Bare wood should be sealed and filled. If the wood has knots or sap streaks, such as those found in several species of pine, these areas should be cleaned with solvent, then sealed with a shellac wash coat to prevent the resins from mixing with the finish coat and bleeding through the topcoat. Lightly sand the shellac wash coat when completely dry. After these areas have been treated and the surface properly sealed and filled, an undercoat should be applied.

An undercoat serves as a primer. When a commercially prepared undercoat is applied to a wood surface, it seals the wood to provide a good surface for the paint or enamel. The undercoat will sand well to provide an excellent bond with the additional coats to be applied. It covers stains and dark areas evenly. Colors will be truer, and less finish coats may be needed.

Thoroughly mix the undercoat. Dip a two-inch quality varnish brush into the undercoat no more than one third the bristle length. Brush undercoat in all directions. Tip off excess undercoat by brushing with a nearly dry brush in the direction of the grain. Allow this smooth, even coat to dry 24 hours. Another coat of undercoat can be applied if necessary. Sand lightly between coats.

5. *Enamel creates a colorful, durable surface that hides wood grain.*

Paints and enamels are applied in the same manner as varnishes. Generally two coats are adequate, but a smoother, glossier surface may be obtained by applying three or four thin coats. The procedure for applying a paint or enamel is as follows:

1. Prepare surface as described above. A smooth clean surface during each phase of application is essential to a successful finish.
2. When the undercoated surface is completely dry, sand lightly with a very fine abrasive. Rub in one direction only. (Because of the opacity of the finish, grain will not be evident.)
3. Use a high-quality soft-bristle varnish brush, either 2 or 2½ inches wide.
4. Dip the brush into the paint or enamel no more than ½ the bristle length. Flow the finish onto the surface freely and evenly. The first coat can

6. *Lightly sand the undercoat with a very fine abrasive.*

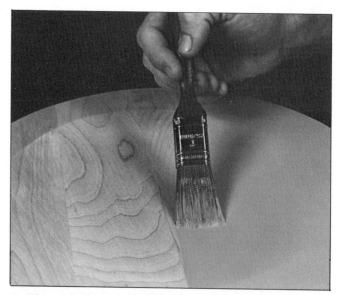

7. *Flow the enamel onto the surface freely and evenly.*

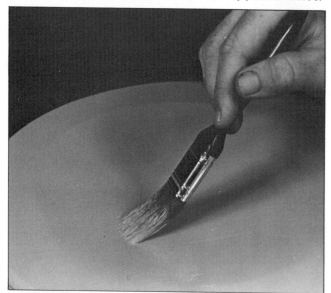

8. *Work the enamel in all directions to ensure uniform coverage.*

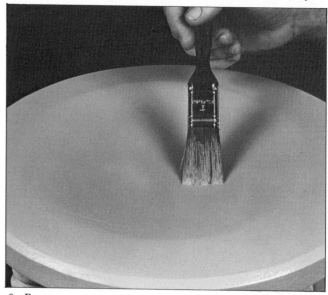

9. *Remove excess enamel by tipping off with a dry brush.*

be thinned slightly.

5. Work the enamel or paint in all directions to ensure even coverage.

6. Dry the brush slightly and go over the surface with straight, light strokes to remove any excess paint or enamel and smooth out the finish.

7. Allow the surface to dry 12 to 24 hours.

8. When dry, sand the surface with finishing garnet "wet or dry" paper, soaked in benzene. This will remove any trace of dust or brush marks. Clean surface with tack rag.

9. Apply additional coats as desired, sanding carefully between coats. Allow the final coat to dry 24 hours.

10. The final finish can be rubbed with pumice stone and water, lightly steel wooled, or left as it is, depending upon the final sheen desired.

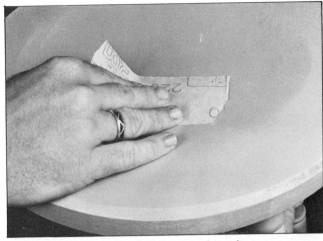

12. Lightly sand the dried enamel surface to remove brush marks.

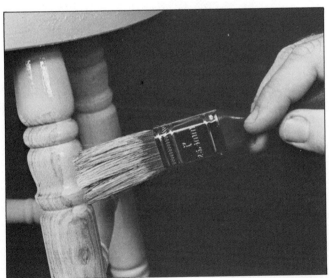

10. Brush around turnings. Tip off to remove excess enamel.

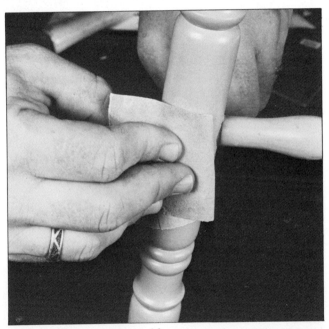

13. Sand all turnings and legs.

11. A nail pounded into each chair leg allows brushing around leg bottom.

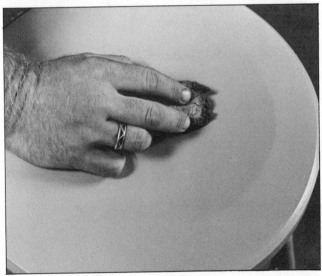

14. Rub the finished surface with steel wool or pumice and oil to the desired sheen.

Rubbing, Waxing, and Polishing

After a finish has been applied to a wood surface and allowed to dry completely, the final finishing step is to rub, wax, or polish the finish to the desired appearance and smoothness. Almost any gloss finish can be rubbed and polished, including varnish, shellac, lacquer, enamel, and polyurethane.

Because most finishes are applied with a brush or rag, the surface finish may dry unevenly in areas. Dust, dirt, and lint can settle on a freshly applied finish and become trapped in the final coat. Rubbing and polishing will create a more uniform smoothness and shine by leveling high spots and removing surface imperfections. Most finishing materials dry to a highly reflective gloss finish. This was desirable many years ago, but the preference today, for contemporary or modern furniture styles, is a finish that is dull or satin in appearance. This is accomplished by rubbing and polishing. If you desire a high-gloss shine, rubbing and polishing will achieve this effect as well.

Rubbing is a process whereby part of the surface is worn away by rubbing with an abrasive without damaging the protective film. Several abrasives can be used, depending upon the appearance desired. Polishing, quite different from rubbing, involves applying a material to the surface, generally a liquid, which seals in the finish oils and renews the shine produced by rubbing when it becomes dull. Polish cleans the surface and can be rubbed to the desired luster. Waxing produces a thicker, more long-lasting protective coat than polishing. Waxing does not clean the surface.

Rubbing

Several abrasive materials can be used to rub a finished surface. Each will produce a specific effect. Whether rubbing between coats or rubbing the final topcoat, allow sufficient time for the finish to dry and harden properly. Rubbing between coats will provide a smooth, slightly scuffed surface for the next coat to adhere to. The abrasives used for rubbing include:

- Sandpaper—not as acceptable as steel wool. Use only superfine grades (600 grit or above). Wet sanding is generally preferable to dry sanding.
- Steel wool—use only superfine grades (3/0).
- Pumice stone—use grades FF or FFF for rubbing. Pumice is an abrasive powder created by crushing volcanic rock. Sift before using.
- Rottenstone—similar to pumice but finer. Available in only one grade.

Several other rubbing supplies will be needed for successful rubbing. Rubbing oil is mixed with pumice or rottenstone as a lubricant. Suitable rubbing oils include raw linseed oil, mineral oil, or paraffin oil. Water can be substituted on occasion for oil. Oil is harder to use because of the residue it leaves on the surface, but dust is much less of a problem. Water is faster and cleaner. A rubbing felt pad is used to cushion the cutting action of the pumice or rottenstone particles. An old toothbrush can be used for carvings, intricate turnings, and other hard-to-reach areas. A clean felt eraser will also do an adequate job. You

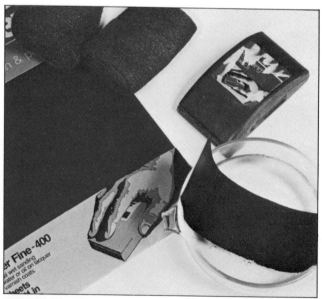

Wet sanding materials.

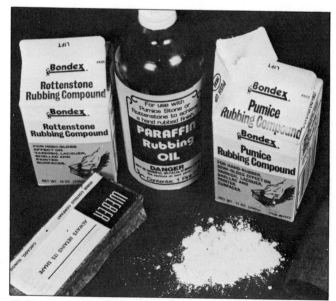

Rubbing materials.

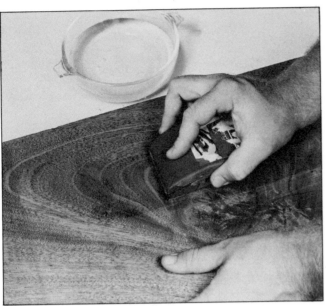

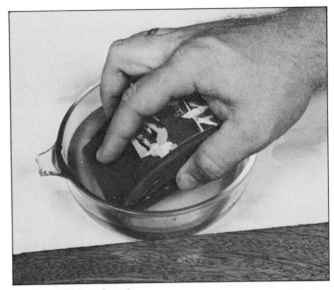

2. *Resoak the abrasive.*

1. *Begin sanding with moderate pressure in direction of the grain.*

should also have benzene or naphtha on hand to remove any oil residue or abrasive particles after rubbing.

Always try to rub in the direction of the grain. Use straight, smooth strokes with uniform pressure. Use the following rubbing techniques to create the desired luster.

Rubbing with Sandpaper—Dull Finish The major problem with sandpaper is that deep scratches that cannot be repaired may be cut into the surface. A variety of sandpaper grades can be used. A superfine sandpaper (8/0 or 10/0) will produce very fine scratches that will create a dull to satin finish. Coarser papers will create a duller, flatter finish.

Oil or water can be used as the lubricant. Do not use water on a shellac finish. Only use aluminum oxide paper with water. Garnet paper is preferred with oil.

1. Soak a section of abrasive paper in rubbing oil or water.
2. Begin sanding with moderate pressure in the direction of the grain. Sandpaper cuts rapidly, so check progress frequently.
3. Resoak the abrasive and continue rubbing until surface has smooth, dull appearance, free from all imperfections.
4. Clean surface with a cloth dampened in benzene.

Rubbing with Steel Wool—Satin Finish Steel wool can be used dry or with rubbing oil. It is easy to use, can be used on hard-to-reach areas effectively, and will produce a relatively smooth, soft satin sheen. Steel wool is best used after initial rubbing with abrasive paper is completed. Oil will serve as a polishing agent when used with steel wool.

1. Press steel wool into a palm-sized ball. Soak in oil, if so desired.

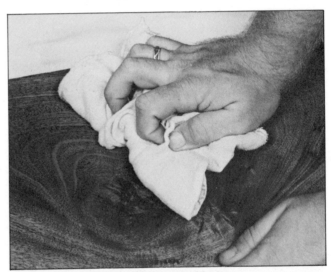

3. *Clean surface with dampened cloth.*

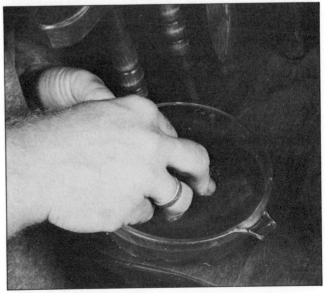

1. *Soak steel wool in oil.*

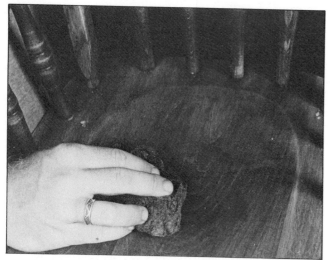

2. Rub surface with steel wool.

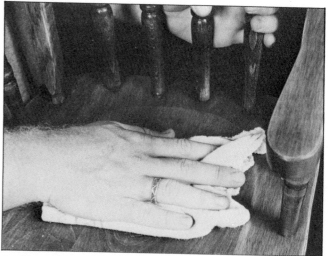

3. Clean with soft cloth.

2. Move steel wool back and forth with moderate pressure in the direction of the grain. Turn steel wool frequently.
3. Rub only until surface imperfections are no longer evident and a soft satin luster is achieved.
4. Clean with soft cloth or brush.
5. Apply polish or wax if desired.

1. Sprinkle pumice on surface.

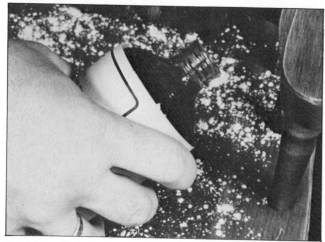

2. Add rubbing oil to surface.

Rubbing with Pumice Stone—Various Lusters Pumice stone is the most widely used rubbing material because it will produce unmatched smoothness and can be used to create a variety of lusters from dull to glossy. Pumice particles are very fine and wear down the surface quickly without producing scratches. Water or oil can be used as the lubricant. Do not dry-rub with pumice stone. Do not use water on a shellac finish. Rubbing with pumice stone should follow rubbing with an abrasive paper or steel wool.

Oil does not cut as rapidly as water which makes it a better lubricant for the finisher with little experience. Oil, however, will produce a film, which must be removed, and requires a much longer drying time. Water as the lubricant will result in a smooth, somewhat dull appearance. Oil will result in greater luster, ranging from satin to semigloss.

1. Use a felt eraser or secure a small sheet of felt to a wooden sanding block. Medium texture felt is best for rubbing.
2. Sprinkle FF- or FFF-grade pumice over the surface to be rubbed.
3. Add lubricant and begin rubbing with felt pad in the direction of the grain. Use even-pressured straight strokes.
4. Add additional lubricant to maintain a rubbing compound of uniform consistency.
5. When a smooth, flat surface with a soft, dull luster is created, the surface is ready for final rubbing after it is completely dry.
6. Clean the surface thoroughly with a wet chamois or a cloth dampened with naphtha or benzene when a water lubricant is used.
7. If FF-grade pumice was used, use FFF-grade pumice, applied in the manner described above, or rottenstone for final rubbing. If FFF was used initially, use rottenstone for final rubbing. Al-

3. Rub with felt pad.

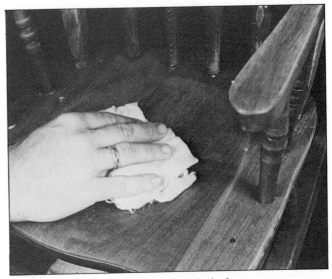

4. Clean with naphtha-dampened cloth.

ways use the same type of lubricant for final rubbing.

Rubbing with Rottenstone—Various Lusters
Since rottenstone is generally used after an initial rubbing with pumice stone, the luster is usually a bit higher than the luster created by the pumice stone. Rottenstone can restore the original high-gloss look of the finish without the wet-looking luster many people find objectionable.

Rottenstone can be used with either water or oil as long as you use the same lubricant that was used on any preceding rubbing. Use a clean felt pad and rub the rottenstone in the same manner as you would the pumice stone. Additional gloss can be achieved by waxing or polishing.

Waxing

Applying a thin coat of wax to a finished surface creates a durable, protective film and rich mellow luster than can be buffed to varying degrees of gloss. Wax improves surface resistance to water and alcohol. A waxed surface also requires less dusting. Wax can be applied over most topcoat finishes or can serve as a finishing material when applied over a stained or bare wood surface.

Wax comes in many forms—paste, cream, liquid, and spray. For a durable protective film though, use only paste wax. Selecting the right wax can be difficult because of the vast number of waxes available. Avoid automotive waxes and self-polishing floor waxes. Hard paste floor waxes are good. Most paste waxes with a relatively high percentage of carnauba wax in the formula are good furniture waxes. Waxes with high percentage of paraffin wax are not nearly as good. Many waxes are formulated with silicone. Silicone adds durability to the wax, but it can make wax difficult to remove.

5. Rub with rottenstone in same manner.

Most commercial wood waxes are combinations of several waxes, thinners, and other ingredients, such as silicone or coloring matter. The major types of waxes are:

- Carnauba wax—the hardest paste wax available. It exhibits excellent polishing characteristics. A good formula is 1 part carnauba wax and 1 part beeswax or 1 part paraffin wax, thinned with turpentine to the proper consistency. Carnauba wax cannot be used alone. It is simply too hard.
- Candelilla wax—not quite as hard as carnauba wax but used in much the same way.
- Beeswax—not as hard as the first two waxes. Has excellent polishing characteristics and is usually thinned 50 percent. Will not attain as high a gloss as the first two waxes.
- Paraffin wax—far softer than other waxes. Serves as a base for most commercial waxes. Can be worked easily but does not possess the hardness and durability of other waxes.

Applying Paste Wax Before applying any wax to a finished surface, the surface must be free of all dust,

1. *Spoon wax onto cloth.*

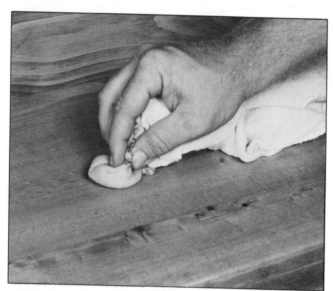

2. *Apply wax to surface with steady circular motion.*

3. *Buff with clean cloth.*

dirt, oil, grease, or previous coats of wax or polish. Clean the surface thoroughly.

1. Spoon paste wax into center of dampened section of clean linen or cheesecloth. Fold cloth around paste wax.

2. Apply wax to the surface, using a circular motion to work the wax both with and across the grain. Do not apply wax thickly.

3. Apply wax only to one section at a time. If you wax too large an area, the wax will set hard and polishing (buffing) will be difficult.

4. Allow the wax about 10 minutes (or the manufacturer's recommended time) to set. Fold a clean section of cheesecloth into a pad and begin buffing in a circular motion. Finish by buffing with long straight strokes in the direction of the grain. Use hard vigorous motion. When you can no longer make a thumbprint on the waxed surface, it is sufficiently polished. The buffing produces a durable protective coating.

5. Allow wax to set 1 hour. Apply additional coats until desired luster is achieved.

Once the surface has been waxed, periodic renewal is necessary to keep the surface looking beautiful. Regular dusting, buffing, and cleaning comprises renewal. Wipe the surface with a damp cloth, buff to restore the desired luster, and if surface dirt or stains are present, clean with a commercial cleaner polish or a cloth slightly dampened with turpentine. When the luster can no longer be restored in this manner, apply more wax.

Wax buildup may become a problem after several applications of wax. Buildup is indicated by a dull or yellow surface, a sticky feel or the excessive buffing that is needed to develop luster. Remove wax buildup by wiping the surface with a cloth dampened with benzene or turpentine.

Polishing

There are hundreds of types and brands of furniture polish on the market. You have undoubtedly noticed the many television commercials for easy-to-apply furniture polishes. Like wax, polishes will give new luster to the finish; however, a polish also cleans as it polishes. The film produced by polish will not last nearly as long as that of a wax, and wax produces a much more durable and protective film.

The most common polishes are oil polishes and liquid-wax polishes. Many are now available in aerosol spray form. Always follow the manufacturer's directions closely when applying these polishes. A thin coat of polish is applied to a finished or waxed surface. The polish picks up dust, dirt, and grime that is removed when the excess polish is wiped away from the surface. A very thin film of polish is left on the surface which can be rubbed or buffed to a high-gloss finish.

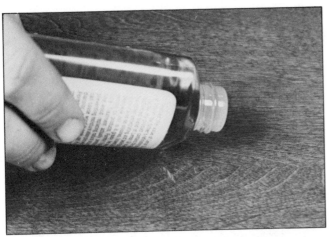

1. *Apply polish to surface.*

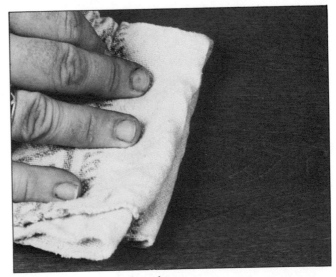

2. *Rub polish around surface.*

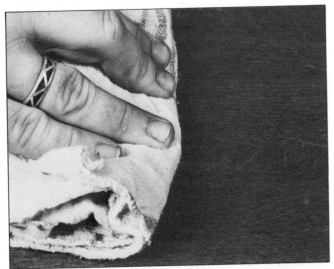

3. *Remove excess polish by wiping in direction of the grain.*

4. *Buff the surface with a circular motion to achieve desired luster.*

These easy-to-use products clean and rejuvenate a surface quickly, but the effects will only last a short time, generally just a few weeks. Apply a polish in the following manner:

1. Shake or mix polish thoroughly.
2. Apply oil polishes to a section of cheesecloth. Spray aerosol polishes onto the furniture surface carefully and sparingly.
3. Spray polishes should be removed immediately from the surface with a clean cloth.
4. Rub oil polishes around in a circular motion, followed by straight strokes in the direction of the grain. Remove excess with brisk strokes in the direction of the grain.
5. Polish the surface with circular buffing action to achieve the desired luster.

Special Decorative Finishes

There are instances when the popular finishing techniques described in the last chapter will not suffice. In these instances, you can select from several intriguing and attractive decorative finishes. Imaginative wood finishers have employed these techniques for many years to set their work apart. These special finishes also can transform inexpensive or damaged furniture into distinctive pieces that become a focal point in a room.

Specialty finishes are a challenge even to the professional wood-finishing craftsman because the results, in many cases, are unpredictable. Mastering a technique can take considerable experimentation, practice, and patience.

Most decorative finishes do not require complete removal of the previous finish, so stripping time can be avoided. Decorative finishes are selected primarily for their beauty. These finishes, by themselves, do not protect the wood surface. Additional coats of a compatible finish are required to bring the surface to sufficient hardness.

Decorative finishes move in and out of vogue, so be prepared to refinish in a few years. Each decorative technique requires a knowledge of wood and the various finishing materials. It is best for the beginner to become familiar with the popular finishing processes and materials discussed in the last chapter before attempting one of these advanced specialty finishes. Because each specialty finish does have its own niche in wood finishing, these techniques will be briefly outlined in this chapter.

Antiquing

Antiquing is one of the most popular specialty finishes today, often referred to as glazing, shading, or highlighting. Antiquing is a relatively simple way to create a mellow, aged appearance that is usually only possible after many years of wear and exposure to the elements.

The effect is achieved by painting a colored glaze over a lighter enamel base coat. When the glaze is carefully wiped away, some of the glaze will remain to highlight turnings, carvings, and even imperfections such as dents or small gouges. The result is a more subdued, mellow appearance that closely resembles that of a one-hundred year-old antique.

Antiquing is easy and does not require much time, even for the beginner. Simply select and apply a good semigloss enamel base coat. When dry, apply a color-coordinated glaze coat. Many paint and hardware stores sell kits that contain everything you need to create a successful antique finish. Some even include brushes and sandpaper. These kits are usually available in traditional color combinations.

Do not antique fine furniture that has wood with good wood-grain patterns and a natural, worn appearance. A clear finish will enhance this wood far more than an antique finish. Wood with interesting contours, spindles, turnings, and carvings will benefit most from an antique finish.

Applying an Antique Finish The surface for an antique finish should be prepared in the same manner as for an enamel finish (described in the last chapter). If the existing finish is in good shape with no sign of peeling or cracking, it does not have to be stripped. Minor damages do not have to be repaired. In fact, many professionals recommend deliberately adding surface blemishes to new unfinished furniture to give the wood a more aged, used appearance. This process is called distressing and will be discussed later.

The base coat is a regular enamel finish. A semigloss sheen works best. Sand the final coat of enamel lightly and clean the surface with a tack cloth. When the enamel base coat has dried completely, begin the glazing process.

If you prefer to show some of the natural wood grain, the base coat can also be a stain. Apply a coat or two of varnish over the stain before applying the glaze.

1. Use a clean dry oil brush to apply a thin coat of glaze on the surface. Use long even strokes with the grain. Too thick a coat will create a strong contrast between base coat and glaze coat.
2. Work the glaze carefully into all cracks, crevices, and blemishes.
3. Break down large project surfaces into convenient areas, and work on one area at a time until the entire surface is covered.
4. Allow the glaze to dry 10 to 20 minutes or until it becomes dull.
5. Begin wiping excess glaze with a clean soft cloth. The success of an antique finish depends on how you wipe down the glaze. Several techniques can be used to produce a wide variety of interesting effects. They will be discussed at the end of this section.

For flat surfaces: Wipe off as much excess glaze as desired with even strokes. Remove all or most of the glaze from the center of the surface, leaving a light film around the edges. Work a dry brush from the lighter center to the edges to create a gradual, barely noticeable change from light to dark. Try to blend the glaze into the lighter center area.

1. *Apply thin coat of glaze, brushing in direction of the grain.*

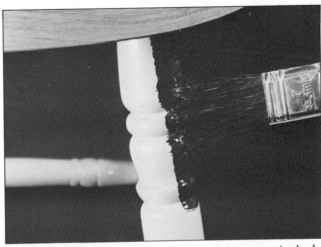

2. *Work glaze into grooves and depressions, particularly on spindles.*

3. *Allow the glaze to dry about 15 minutes or until it appears dull.*

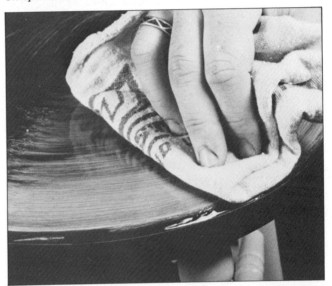

4. *Wipe off glaze with a clean soft cloth. Use light pressure.*

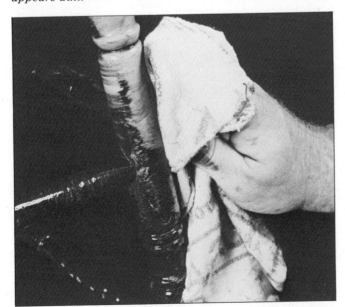

5. *Wipe glaze from elevated areas.*

6. *An antiqued stool leg.*

7. *Apply a protective coat of clear finish. Polyurethane is used here.*

8. *Lightly rub the surface with fine steel wool and apply a coat or two of paste wax.*

For curved and carved surfaces: Wipe excess glaze from the elevated areas with a soft cloth. Using a dry brush blend the glaze trapped in depressions and grooves into the lighter elevated areas to create a gradual change from light to dark. Depressions should appear dark, high spots light, but the transition should be gradual.

6. When you achieve the look you desire, allow the glaze to dry overnight.

7. Apply a protective coat of varnish or shellac depending on the manufacturer's recommendation.

8. Lightly rub with fine steel wool and wax-polish the entire surface.

Special Antiquing Effects Many special effects can be created with a few simple techniques. Most of these effects require little time and effort and can help create a simulated patina. If you are a beginner using one of the following techniques, use a light hand until you develop a feel for the technique.

Distressing True antiques often have mars and surface damages resulting from years of exposure and hard wear. Distressing wood, one of the most popular special techniques, artificially creates these wear marks to make the wood look older than it actually is. Distressing should be done prior to applying any finish coat.

Wear is simulated by intentionally marring the wood surface with tools or household items. Worn edges and high use areas can be simulated by sanding with sandpaper, rasps, or other abrasives. Dents, nicks, and gouges can be created with a wide variety of items. Use your imagination and have some fun. Sand all imperfections well.

Spattering After the glaze coat has dried, you can add spatter marks to the finish by flicking the bristles of a stiff brush. A toothbrush works very well. A good spattering technique will simulate wormholes that

are quire common in old woods. Do not overload the brush. Place your thumb on the bristles and pull back toward you, moving the thumb across the bristles. The spring action will flick specs of paint onto the surface. A flat black paint generally works very well for spattering.

Graining The grain pattern of an uninteresting plain wood can be improved greatly by simulating a grain with glaze. This is intended to be a decorative effect, not an exact duplication of grain pattern. Several manufacturers offer complete graining kits, but, generally, you can find good grain-making tools around the home.

Glaze the wood as you would for antiquing. Before the glaze has a chance to dry, drag the bristles of a dry brush across the surface to create a textured wood appearance. Several comb-type brushes, available at large paint and hardware stores, are excellent tools for creating simulated wood grain. Experiment until you create an acceptable, attractive pattern.

Stippling This decorative technique produces a mottled effect that can be created in several ways. Immediately after applying the glaze coat, lightly touch the surface with a crumpled cloth, paper towel, or dry sponge. This blotting action will produce a variety of patterns.

Stippling can also be accomplished during glazing. Use just the tip of a dry brush to dab a pattern of glaze onto the surface. Touch only the very tips of the bristles to the glaze. Then, using a pouncing motion, apply the glaze to the enameled surface.

Marbleizing Marbleizing is a dramatic, decorative effect used on the top flat surfaces of furniture. The effect can be accomplished in several ways. The easiest method is to crumple plastic wrap, set it on top of a fresh coat of glaze, and press the plastic into the glaze with a cloth. Lift the plastic and you should have a simple marble pattern.

Another marbleizing technique involves spattering blobs of several colored glazes on the enamel surface. The spattering is done in the same manner as described earlier, only use a slightly fuller brush.

Highlighting You can increase the light to dark contrast of antiquing by a technique called highlighting. After applying and wiping the glaze to achieve an antique finish, emphasize the shadows by sanding the glazed areas lightly to make the transition from dark to light even more gradual and subtle.

Gilding and Bronzing

Applying gold to wood, either from thin sheets or from powders, is a decorative technique that dates back to early Egyptian civilization. Gold has long been a symbol of wealth and power, and in recent decades it has been used to decorate fine furniture. This technique is called gilding or frequently called gold leafing.

Gilding is most commonly found on formal English and French furniture from the eighteenth century. It is also widely used on ornate picture frames and moldings.

Today, true gold leaf is incredibly expensive which places gilding out of the financial range of most home refinishers. Because gold leaf is generally less than one four-thousandth of an inch thick, it is also very difficult to apply. Gilding is an expensive, exact, time-consuming art that is best left to the most skilled craftsmen. Volumes have been written about the gilding technique, so we will not attempt to describe the actual technique in a few paragraphs.

Although nothing can compare to the beauty and durability of a piece of gilded furniture, the expense and tremendous amount of work involved can be reduced considerably by using an alternative method which simulates the gilded look. This is achieved by mixing powders (either bronze or gold) into the shellac or varnish to be used for finishing. These powders are available at art stores and paint and hardware stores. The finish must be mixed well and thinned slightly more than normal to compensate for the metallic powder.

The use of metal powders is called bronzing or powder gilding. Although bronzing powders do not hold their color as well as gold leaf does, they are available in a wide range of colors. Follow manufacturer's instructions closely to make sure the bronzing powder you intend to use is chemically compatible with the topcoat you plan to apply. Bronzing powders are generally applied by tapping them onto a tacky surface or by mixing the powder with the clear finish.

Another method, which resembles true gilding even more than bronzing, is called wax gilding. This is probably the most popular gilding method today because it is inexpensive and easy to do. The process simply involves rubbing a paste wax that contains gold flakes onto the wood surface. When buffed to a fine uniform sheen, wax gold closely resembles gold leaf. This is an excellent method for the inexperienced home finisher.

There are also gold leaf liquids that are perfect for highlighting, accenting, or striping. These are metallic paints that can be applied to the areas desired with a small camel's hair paintbrush. All that is necessary is a steady hand. Gold leaf paints should not be used to cover large flat surfaces because the apparent brush marks will detract from the overall beauty.

Decoupage

Decoupage is the ancient decorative technique of fastening a printed image or design to a wood surface. Several coats of clear finish are then applied over the print and surrounding surface to make the image appear as part of the finish. Any kind of image will do: art prints, designs, photos, invitations, announcements, maps, or documents that you value and wish to preserve.

The actual application is quite simple, but a few things should be considered first. The printed image must be clear and printed on only one side, and the paper on which the image is printed must not be very thick. Use only high-quality varnish, shellac, lacquer, or polyurethane as the topcoat.

Cutting out the design can be done in a number of ways. You can remove the entire background by cutting around the main subject with a scissors or razor. You can leave part of the background in to add interest. You can tear out the design to create a soft torn edge. The edges of the design can be scorched or burned away. If the design you intend to use is printed on thick paper, some of the thickness can be removed by moistening the back of the paper and then rolling back layers of the paper with the fingers. Allow the design to dry thoroughly.

The application technique is as follows:

1. The bare wood surface must be completely smooth and clean. Prepare raw wood surface as you would for any other finish. Seal and fill the surface properly.

2. Decoupage can be applied to bare wood, stained wood, or wood that has been painted. Select a background color that will enhance the design you have selected. Stain the surface, if you so desire; or if you prefer an opaque color, paint 2 or more coats of enamel on the surface. If you plan to apply the design to bare wood, first apply a thin coat of finish material. Make sure the base will be compatible with the final finish you intend to use. Allow the surface to dry completely. Lightly

sand the surface to increase smoothness.

3. Spread a thin coat of diluted white glue to the back of the printed design. Position the design carefully on the prepared wood surface. Place a piece of plastic kitchen wrap over the design (never use wax paper). Use a roller to securely fasten the design to the wood and to squeeze excess glue from beneath the design. Wipe with a damp cloth. Repeat the plastic wrap-roll-wipe sequence until no more excess glue exists. Allow to dry overnight.

4. Should bubbles appear when dry, slit them and apply glue to back with a toothpick. Repeat last portion of Step 3.

5. Apply a thin coat of diluted glue to the front of the design. This acts as a sealer. Allow to dry.

6. Begin applying clear finish coats, using the technique described in the previous chapter for your specific finish. Satin and gloss finishes work best. Plan on applying 7 to 15 coats. Apply 4 or 5 coats of finish, then wet sand with very fine abrasive paper. Keep applying coats of clear finish and sanding until an adequate protective coat is built up. Top with a coat of paste wax.

1. Cut out design carefully.

2. Apply glue to back of design.

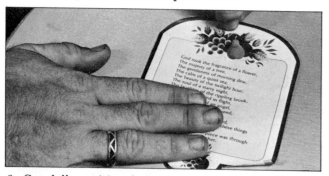

3. Carefully position design.

4. Secure to surface with roller.

5. Clean with damp cloth.

6. Apply glue to front of design.

7. Apply several coats of finish (left).

Finish Maintenance and Repairs

A furniture finish that receives proper care and maintenance will retain its natural beauty and protect the wood beneath it for a long time. With the advent of the new synthetic finishes that are harder and more durable than traditional wood finishes, it is easy to neglect the finish once it's applied. Even the most durable finishes, however, occasionally become dull or damaged and require restoration. The longer a finish does not receive proper care, the harder restoration becomes.

A regular maintenance program will keep your finish in top form. The best maintenance, of course, is preventive maintenance. Treat any wooden object with care. Many of the conditions that harm a finished wood surface can be minimized or avoided. Keeping a wood finish in good condition is relatively easy.

- Even well-seasoned wood will be affected by drastic changes in temperature and humidity. Dry conditions can shrink wood; humid or wet conditions will cause the wood to swell. Prolonged humidity will destroy a shellac or paste wax finish. It is impossible to control the weather, but control the environment as best you can to avoid extremes.
- Scratches, gouges, dents, burns, and other damages can be eliminated to a large degree by using common sense. Keep fine furniture away from heavy traffic areas. Isolated corners offer greatest protection. Use pads on top of furniture during heavy use periods, such as parties or moving day. Always supply coasters and ashtrays to guests. Pad with felt the bottoms of all lamps and other objects that rest on furniture. Use furniture only for its intended purpose—a dining room table is not a workbench.
- Liquids can cause damage to most finishes. Wipe up all spills immediately. Place coasters under all drinks or pitchers to prevent rings from forming on the finished surface.
- Heat can destroy a finish in seconds. Never set hot objects directly on a finished surface. Use asbestos heat pads or serve from an adjacent counter.

No matter how much preventive care you give a finish, it will still become dull and dirty from the accumulation of dust and dirt. For this reason, periodic cleaning, waxing, and polishing are necessary.

Dusting is probably the easiest way to maintain a beautiful wood finish. Dust is fairly easy to recognize. Determine how long it takes for dust to build up. Then dust regularly at this interval. Never dry dust. Dampen a soft cloth slightly with water or lemon oil and wipe lightly in the direction of the grain. Avoid overuse of wax-based aerosol sprays that claim to wax as you clean. This material quickly builds up into a dull, somewhat opaque film that is hard to remove.

Dusting generally keeps wood surfaces clean; however, a thin coat of grime and grease may gradually build up on the surface despite regular dusting. To remove this accumulation, you will have to use a specially formulated cleaner. Soap and warm water will generally remove grime from a waterproof finish. Do not use water on wood that may be fastened with water-soluble glues. A wax finish can be cleaned with a cloth dampened with turpentine. There are many commercial cleaners, all of which will do an adequate job provided you check the label to make sure the cleaner can be used on the finish you plan to clean.

Restoring a Damaged Finish

Before you can repair minor finish damages, you must first determine the type of finish. This is not a problem provided you applied the finish. If you did not apply the existing finish, identification can be difficult. Remove any wax with a cloth dampened with benzene or turpentine. Identify the finish according to the following characteristics:

- Shellac: Rub an unexposed area of the finish with a cloth dampened with denatured alcohol. If the finish dissolves, it is shellac.
- Varnish: The only solvent that will dissolve varnish is a paint or varnish remover. Apply some to an unexposed area and see if the finish dissolves.
- Lacquer: Rub lacquer thinner on an unexposed area of the finish. If the area looks worn or scuffed, then dries to a smooth glossy finish, the finish is most likely lacquer.
- Polyurethane: This finish will resist most solvents. If you try all of the above solvents without success, the finish is probably polyurethane. You can try to dissolve the finish with a special synthetic solvent.
- Penetrating resin or rubbed oil: You can identify these finishes by appearance. The grain can be seen and felt. The surface is not coated with a clear protective film.

Once you identify the finish, you can make all necessary repairs. Some repair techniques vary for different finishes. In the following section, common surface damages to the finish will be presented along with their respective repair techniques. Try to repair damages shortly after they happen.

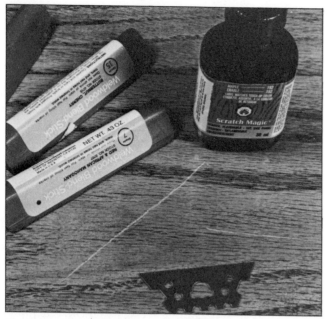

Scratched finishes can be repaired in a number of ways.

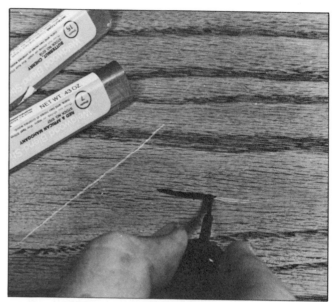

1. Apply commercial scratch fluid.

2. Allow the commercial preparation to dry for a few minutes.

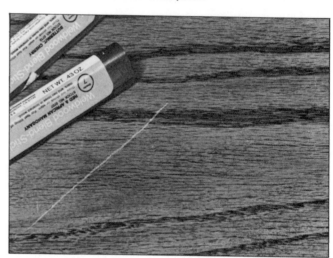

3. When the preparation is wiped from the surface, the scratch is no longer visible.

Scratches Small shallow scratches can usually be removed by a process called reamalgamation (discussed in the next section). Wax sticks or even nail polish will also conceal such scratches on most finishes. Commercially prepared wax sticks or wax crayons can be used. Melt the wax and allow it to drip into the scratch. Force the material into the scratch and smooth with a heated knife. If these methods do not remove the scratch or if the scratch is quite deep, the blemish will have to be filled and colored. This is most effectively done with shellac sticks. Shellac-stick application requires practice. Select a stick closest to the color of the finish. Melt the shellac and work it into the scratch with a heated knife. Shave off excess shellac with a razor blade when dry. Rub the surface with fine steel wool.

Scrapes Wide scrapes require refinishing of the damaged area. Filler and stain must be replaced if the scrape has damaged both finish and wood. Refinish the damaged surface with the proper finish and technique.

Gouges and Burns These are severe damages that may require complete refinishing. Unless these damages are shallow surface blemishes, which they usually are not, they are too extensive to be repaired with shellac or wax sticks. Gouges or burns that extend well into the actual wood surface will have to be cleaned (scrape all of the charred edges of a burn with a knife), filled with wood putty, sanded, and finished with stick shellac or topcoat finish. This procedure is described in greater detail in the wood preparation chapter.

White Spots, Rings, or Blushing When finishes are exposed to moisture, either prolonged periods of humidity or by setting liquids on the finish, white spots, rings, or clouded areas may form. These blemishes generally only form on or in the finish, so complete refinishing is seldom needed. Blushing or cloudy areas can usually be removed by rubbing the blemish

1. *A deep scratch can be filled with a wax stick or crayon.*

2. *After the scratch is filled, scrape off excess with a razor blade.*

3. *Rub repaired area lightly with very fine steel wool.*

Cloudy white areas are fairly common finish damages that are often repaired by rubbing.

with pumice stone and oil. White spots or rings are the most common damage to finishes. The whiter the blemish, the deeper the damage. Try one of the following methods to remove these blemishes:

- Rub with pumice stone and oil.
- Sprinkle cigar ashes on the area and rub with a cloth dampened with oil.
- Rub with oil and salt.
- Apply a mild ammonia-water solution.
- Purchase a commercial preparation intended for this problem.

Dark Spots and Stains Dark stains mean trouble. They can be caused by water or moisture that has penetrated through the finish, discoloring the wood beneath it. These stains usually require complete refinishing, so you have nothing to lose by trying to repair the stained area. Remove the finish above and around the spot by sanding with abrasive paper.

Bleach the stained wood with ammonia, household bleach, or an oxalic acid solution, according to the technique described in an earlier chapter. Apply several times until the stain matches the surrounding wood color. If bleaching does not remove the stain, the stain must be sanded or scraped away. If bleaching lightens the wood too much, stain the wood the proper color. Refinish to match surrounding surface. If this method does not work, a complete refinishing must be done.

1. Rub with pumice and oil.

Worn Finishes A wood finish that is exposed to repeated heavy use may wear thin in several areas. Worn areas appear dull, scuffed, and scratched. If the finish is not worn completely away, simply overcoat the area with a compatible finish. In some heavy-use areas, the finish may be completely worn away. In many cases the wood will have to be restained to match the surrounding surface. Clean the worn area well. Lightly sand the area. Apply a proper wash coat to seal the wood. Stain to match. Apply several coats of finish. Rub to match surrounding sheen.

Cracks and Alligatoring When the wood beneath a finish expands and contracts with drastic temperature changes, the finish develops a complex series of cracks. This is another problem that generally requires complete refinishing, but repair is worth a try. If the cracks are not exceptionally deep, reamalgamation may eliminate the problem.

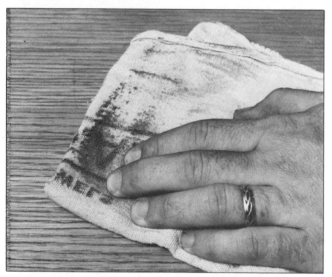

2. Wipe with naphtha-dampened rag.

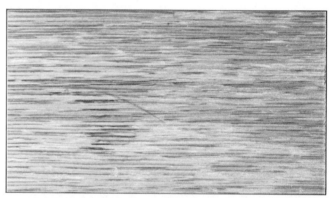

1. A badly worn finish.

2. Sand area with steel wool.

3. The cloudy area is removed.

3. Apply a coat of original finish.

Reviving an Old Finish

Many times an old piece of furniture or wood appears to need refinishing; however many drab and dull finishes can be restored without stripping off the existing finish. The rich mellow character of aged wood can easily be destroyed during the stripping process. Reviving the finish will retain the patina of the wood while creating a finish that will look nearly as good as a new finish. Reviving a finish requires only a fraction of the time, money, and effort refinishing would require. Before reviving a finish, clean the surface well, identify the existing finish, and repair all damages.

There are four basic revival methods: abrasion, reamalgamation, overcoating, and padding. Each of these techniques is easy to do and requires very little time.

- Abrasion: Very fine steel wool is used to remove spots, rings, and dull areas that have not penetrated through the finish to the bare wood. Many times, blemishes have penetrated very little. Rubbing with fine steel wool or even pumice stone and oil will wear away the blemish, leaving the remaining finish intact. Never use abrasive papers as they cut through the finish very quickly.
- Reamalgamation: This is a very simple process of applying the finish's solvent to the surface with a brush or very fine steel wool. Before the solvent evaporates, brush or rub the solvent around the surface quickly until surface blemishes disappear. Apply a light coat of solvent to the surface and brush or rub in the direction of the grain to smooth out the entire surface. When dry, rub the surface with very fine steel wool. Apply a coat of paste wax.
- Overcoating: In some cases the finish is too thin for the above methods to work. The finish on high-use areas of older furniture may be completely

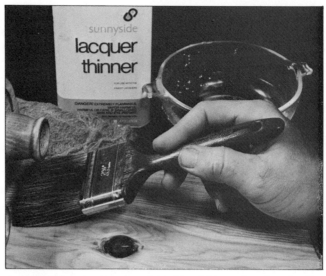

1. Reamalgamation involves brushing solvent onto the surface to dissolve and smooth the finish.

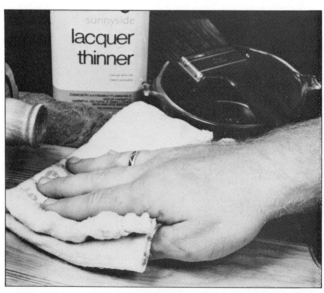

2. Carefully and quickly rub the solvent around the surface to ensure uniform coverage.

Abrasion with very fine steel wool will remove many minor finish damages.

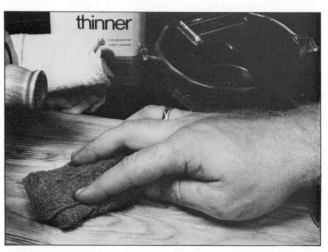

3. Rub the surface with very fine steel wool. Apply coat of wax.

worn away. Clean the surface, repair any blemishes, and rub the surface lightly with fine steel wool. Overcoating is the process of applying a new coat(s) of finish over an existing finish. Varnish is a popular overcoating material. Apply the overcoating finish as you would apply a new coat of finish.

- Padding: This method requires a hard-to-find material called padding lacquer. Padding materials can usually be ordered from a finishing supply house. A soft cotton pad is used to apply the padding lacquer. Always keep the pad moving, never allowing it to rest on the surface. This action creates a high-gloss finish that can be dulled, if desired, by rubbing with fine steel wool.

- There are also several commercial preparations that will revive most finishes. The manufacturer's instructions must be followed carefully. Commercial refinishes are actually very similar to reamalgamation.

The following chart describes how to revive finishes.

Reviving Popular Finishes

SHELLAC	• Remove protective paste wax coat, if any. • Rub surface with pumice stone and oil to remove top, dull layer and smooth the surface. • Apply 1 or 2 new coats of shellac. Varnish, lacquer, and some polyurethanes can be used. They offer a harder, more durable finish.
VARNISH	• Clean surface thoroughly. • Reamalgamation works well on varnish finishes. • Mix 1 part turpentine with 2 or 3 parts boiled linseed oil, and apply solution to varnish surface with a clean cloth, using a circular motion followed by strokes in the direction of the wood grain. • Rub until all blemishes have been removed. • Buff surface and apply a coat of paste wax.
LACQUER	• Use reamalgamation to restore a lacquer finish. • Clean surface thoroughly. • Using long even strokes across the grain, apply lacquer thinner to surface. • Brush over it in the direction of the grain. • A few coats may be required.
RUBBED OIL & PENETRATING RESIN	• Clean surface thoroughly. • Mix 1 part turpentine with 3 parts boiled linseed oil and apply to surface. • Allow to penetrate 15 to 20 minutes and buff the surface. • Apply several coats until a desirable finish is achieved.
POLYURETHANE	• Clean surface thoroughly. • Use abrasion to smooth surface. • Reapply 1 or 2 coats of original finish.

Waxing and Polishing

Applying wax or polish to a wood finish will impart a smooth, deep shine and protect the surface for a reasonably long period of time. After you clean a finish, apply one of the many commercial polishes according to the manufacturer's recommendations. Most of these products are quite easy to use and are available in two basic forms—cream or liquid. An excellent finish polish can be made by mixing equal parts of boiled linseed oil and turpentine.

Apply any polish liberally, and briskly run it over the surface in a circular motion with firm even pressure. Remove any excess polish with a clean dry cloth. Buff the finish to the desired sheen.

Sometimes a finish may require a new application of wax. Wax lasts much longer and produces a more mellow shine than does polish. Waxing is necessary only when the previous coat of wax can no longer be renewed by buffing with a soft clean cloth. Too many coats of wax will product a wax buildup. Apply wax only a few times each year. Wax buildup is dull and yellow, will not buff easily, and results in a gummy surface—particularly in hot, humid conditions. Buildup can be removed with a cloth dampened in benzene.

The following chart indicates how to care for each of the popular finishes:

Wood Finish Maintenance Chart

Finish	Protection	Cleaner	Polish
Shellac	Apply several coats of paste wax to build up a strong protective, waterproof coat	Nonalcohol base commercial cleaner formulated for use on a shellac finish	Standard furniture polish
Varnish	Apply a coat of paste wax—apply additional coats as needed	Mild soap and water	Equal parts of boiled linseed oil and turpentine or a commercial polish
Lacquer	Apply a coat of paste wax—apply additional coats as needed	Commercial cleaner formulated for use on lacquer	Standard furniture polish
Penetrating Resin	Apply additional coats of penetrating resin for additional protection	Mild soap and water	Not necessary
Rubbed Oil	Apply additional coats of oil for additional protection	Commercial cleaner formulated for use on rubbed oil	Not necessary
Polyurethane	Apply a coat of paste wax—apply additional coats as needed	Mild soap and water	Equal parts of boiled linseed oil and turpentine or a commercial polish
Paint and Enamel	Apply a coat of paste wax—apply additional coats as needed	Mild soap and water	Standard furniture polish

Index